T0287087

CLASSICAL CROSSROADS

CLASSICAL CROSSROADS

The Path Forward
for Music in the 21st Century

LEONARD SLATKIN

AMADEUS
PRESS

Lanham • Boulder • New York • London

Published by Amadeus Press
An imprint of The Rowman & Littlefield Publishing Group, Inc.
4501 Forbes Boulevard, Suite 200, Lanham, Maryland 20706
www.rowman.com

6 Tinworth Street, London SE11 5AL, United Kingdom

Copyright © 2021 by The Rowman & Littlefield Publishing Group, Inc.

All rights reserved. No part of this book may be reproduced in any form or by
any electronic or mechanical means, including information storage and retrieval
systems, without written permission from the publisher, except by a reviewer
who may quote passages in a review.

British Library Cataloguing in Publication Information Available

Library of Congress Cataloging-in-Publication Data

Names: Slatkin, Leonard, author.
Title: Classical crossroads : the path forward for music in the 21st
    century / Leonard Slatkin.
Description: Lanham : Amadeus Press, 2021. | Includes bibliographical
    references and index.
Identifiers: LCCN 2021003791 (print) | LCCN 2021003792 (ebook) | ISBN
    9781538152225 (cloth) | ISBN 9781538152232 (epub)
Subjects: LCSH: Orchestra—History—21st century. | Music trade. | COVID-19
    (Disease)—Social aspects. | Slatkin, Leonard.
Classification: LCC ML1208 .S53 2021 (print) | LCC ML1208 (ebook) | DDC
    784.209/05—dc23
LC record available at https://lccn.loc.gov/2021003791
LC ebook record available at https://lccn.loc.gov/2021003792

♾️™ The paper used in this publication meets the minimum requirements of
American National Standard for Information Sciences—Permanence of Paper
for Printed Library Materials, ANSI/NISO Z39.48-1992.

For my son, Daniel,
with love, friendship, and music

Only on paper has humanity yet achieved glory, beauty, truth, knowledge, virtue, and abiding love.

—George Bernard Shaw

The function of music is to release us from the tyranny of conscious thought.

—Sir Thomas Beecham

Why are there trees I never walk under but large and melodious thoughts descend upon me?

—Walt Whitman

All that is valuable in human society depends upon the opportunity for development accorded the individual.

—Albert Einstein

Thank you, ladies and gentlemen, for your magnificent indifference.

—Dizzy Gillespie

CONTENTS

INTRODUCTION

> What we call the beginning is often the end. And to
> make an end is to make a beginning. The end is where
> we start from.
>
> —T. S. Eliot

On September 1, 2019, I turned seventy-five, a day filled with
lovely notes and messages, a couple of surprises, and a lot of
reflection. Among the first of my mini epiphanies was the realization
that I had been conducting for almost sixty years. Questions began
to form in my mind, mostly regarding what has changed since I first
began my baton-wielding journey.

Changes are inevitable, and those that took place over this time
in the classical music workplace were extraordinary. Still, if we were
to travel back to the middle of the 19th century, we would find that
a lot of concert life was the same then as it is these days. An orchestra would usually perform a program that started with an overture,
continued with a concerto, and concluded with a symphony. Concerts would include premieres, revivals of lesser-known pieces, and
star soloists. We have seen variations on that theme over the years,
but for the most part, we have continued to be content with that
presentation format.

The turn of the 21st century saw more music reaching a broader
audience. Recordings, video technology, and the internet had a lot
to do with it, as one could even see full-length operas, plays, and
ballets in the movie theater or at home.

As a result of such developments, the relevance of classical art forms has been called into question. Do we really need symphony orchestras anymore? Why does it seem as if there is an endless cycle of repetition in what the audiences hear? With technology leaping over itself almost by the minute, is there really a place for what used to be called "high culture"? Why are our school systems leaving the arts out of the curriculum?

My first two books, *Conducting Business* and *Leading Tones,* were primarily about my life, with observations regarding musical matters and how to lead an orchestra. For this volume, I have selected certain topics that are relevant to the musical world today. Dedicating a chapter to each subject, I address matters within the theme that puzzle me and offer suggestions about how to solve those particular dilemmas.

How do we cope with the lack of diversity in the classical music workforce? Are our concert venues too large to accommodate the downturn in audience size? Do we have a one-size-fits-all type of orchestral sonority due to a broken system of auditions? Who actually runs our organizations?

When COVID-19 changed the global landscape, the musical scene changed dramatically as well. With no work or travel to occupy my time, I began to think about possibilities for the industry that might exist both during and after the pandemic. As the weeks dragged on, I found my writing taking on a different tone, almost angry at times. Instead of my usual monthly web essays detailing my travel exploits and conducting activities, I started a journal devoted to the ways we are dealing with the virus in the arts world.

The series took on a life of its own. In rereading these posts, I decided to include several of them in this volume. As the pandemic progressed, this section became the largest topic of discussion in the book. Several of the ideas might apply well after we have the virus under control. And perhaps by the time you read this, the arts industry will have dealt with many of the difficulties facing cultural organizations in this changed world.

I have incorporated a few amusing stories along the way, but only to clarify a point. The general tone of this book is one of serious intent. However, there is one feature that is quite new.

As I was writing, it occurred to me that I wanted to involve the reader in a different way, so I set up a system that allowed visitors to my website to participate in the process. Every week, I posted a topic on my homepage and social media channels, inviting readers to pose questions to me based on a brief description in the hope that they might point me in a new direction. Although some subjects elicited more responses than others, I received many thought-provoking comments and several that were a bit contentious. Those I chose to integrate into the book added intriguing ingredients to an already busy stew.

It is not possible to cover everything, but I hope that some of the ideas presented might help as we all try to figure out what to do next to make the world a better place through the arts. We learn from the past to create a better future. Perhaps a few baby steps are contained in the pages you are about to read.

With three-quarters of a century behind me, I can only thank those who have made my life such a wonderful adventure. It has been a great honor to be in the service of music, working alongside others who engage and inspire communities through the arts. In particular, I would like to give thanks to my wife, Cindy McTee, my executive assistant, Leslie Karr, as well as the dedicatee of this book, my son Daniel.

I

FIRST MOVEMENT

1

ON CONDUCTING

No statement should be believed because it is made by
an authority.

—Robert A. Heinlein

In 1925, Richard Strauss wrote a short essay offering career advice
for conductors:

TEN GOLDEN RULES
Written in the scrapbook of a young conductor

1. Remember that you do not make music for your own amuse-
   ment, but for the pleasure of your audience.
2. Do not perspire when conducting; only the public ought to
   get warm.
3. Conduct *Salome* and *Elektra* as if they were by Mendelssohn;
   fairy-music.
4. Never look at the brass encouragingly; except with a quick
   glance for an important lead-in.
5. On the contrary, never let the horns and woodwind out of
   your sight; if you hear them at all they are already too loud.
6. If you think the brass is not strong enough, tone them down
   two points further.
7. It is not enough yourself to hear every word of the singer—
   which you know by heart anyway; the public also must be
   able to follow it without effort. If they don't understand what
   is happening they fall asleep.

8. Always accompany the singer so as to enable him to sing without exertion.
9. If you think you have reached the utmost Prestissimo, take the tempo as fast again.
10. If you remember all this sympathetically, your rich talents and great knowledge will always be the unimpaired delight of your audience.[1]

When we watch available videos of this great composer, we can infer that perhaps he is, of course, being facetious in some of his commandments. What we do not know is how he spent his time in rehearsal, which is where the work gets accomplished. As Strauss suggests, the performance is meant to please the listeners, and not to distract them with exaggerated mannerisms.

But that was a century ago, and times have changed. These days, I believe that we need a few more rules by which to be governed. There is no conductors' legislative bureau, so we have to fend for ourselves. Nevertheless, unlike in Strauss's time, we are held accountable to some stringent regulations imposed upon us by orchestras and unions. These must be obeyed, and as I will say often in this book, "The clock is the enemy of the conductor."

With that in mind, as well as my own set of experiences at the podium, I offer these additional suggestions to add to the German maestro's list:

1. Do not talk too much. Orchestras only need to know six things: faster or slower, louder or softer, and shorter or longer. That's all. Everything else is a variation on those themes. How can this be? Look at the next rule.
2. Try to get an engagement with an orchestra that is in a country where you do not speak one word of the language. These days, there are always musicians who can communicate in English, no matter where in the world you are. Still, as a conductor, you are reduced, automatically, to keeping your remarks short and to the point. Your stick, eyes, and body do the work, not your mouth.
3. When you arrive at the first rehearsal, look around and make sure that you know where everyone is situated in the

orchestra. Few oversights are more embarrassing than giving a cue in one direction, only to have the sound come from another. Each orchestra has its own stage plot, and it is more than helpful to find out who is where.

4. Check when the break occurs in the rehearsal and how long it lasts. This helps in planning what you will do during the rehearsal and gives you some idea about how to control the time you spend on each piece. More than one conductor has not been given this information and has run out of minutes before completing what he or she had planned.

5. Make sure the music stand is at the correct height. Yes, this seems obvious, but you would be surprised by the number of conductors who just plunge right in, only to discover that they have to lean forward more than expected to turn the page. Ask a stagehand to help, or even a member of the orchestra.

6. Learn where your dressing room is. When you come to the stage door, someone needs to take you to your quarters, but that will only occur on the first day. Sometimes the backstage area is like a labyrinth, involving multiple floors and staircases connected by long corridors. It is often equally difficult to get out of the building. That leads us to:

7. Figure out how to get to the stage. Certainly you will be accompanied the first time. But there are things to remember as you make your way to the podium. Is it on the same floor as the dressing room? Are there photos on the wall that you can use as a map? Will you enter the stage from the right or left side? If you are in doubt, ask one of the musicians to point the way. If they like you, it is possible you will be directed to the correct spot.

8. You do not have to know the orchestra musicians' names. It would certainly be impressive if you could call on them individually, but just identifying the instrument or chair will suffice. They will call you Maestro or Maestra. Do not take this as anything more than the title you have for the time you are there. Most of us do not really deserve this appellation anyway.

9. Avoid making faces when something goes wrong. Assume that it was something you did that caused the error in the first place.

10. Always show the love you have for the music, even if you hate it. We have all done pieces that we did not want to perform, but for the time that we are working on it, the composition must be thought of as the finest ever written.

11. When working with singers, in particular, avoid wearing strong perfume or cologne. You might need something if you have a tendency to perspire, but go easy on the scent.

12. When you are conducting, imagine that you are playing somewhere in the back of the second violins. That is the correct volume for speaking to the orchestra. Everyone needs to hear what you are going to say, particularly when you are telling them where to start up again.

13. Wait for the musicians to be ready before giving any beat. Getting the attention of all players is crucial, otherwise you will have to start over. But you also must be aware of who is playing at the place where you will commence. There is no point waiting for the first violins at the start of *Ein Heldenleben.*

14. At the first rehearsal, always try to play through one piece without stopping. The orchestra has to get to know you and vice versa. Do not begin with the most difficult new work but rather something that you know can be read with relative ease. Take mental notes on what works and what does not.

15. Use the first day to plan how you will organize the next rehearsals. Keep in mind that the clock is ready to stop you, so prepare accordingly.

16. On the day or evening of the performance, double check that you have everything you need for the concert. Often, conductors tend to forget things such as suspenders, ties, handkerchiefs, and even shoes.[2]

17. Do not make the management sweat. Get to the venue at least fifteen minutes before showtime. And always remember that there are at least twenty members of the orchestra

who can conduct this program, perhaps even better than
you.

18. At the conclusion of a piece of music, give the musicians
who had prominent solos a bow. It is easy in a piece like
Prelude to the Afternoon of a Faun but complicated for *Boléro*.
I leave it to you to figure out, but don't be concerned if you
forgot someone and he or she is knocking at your dressing
room door.

19. Always give the orchestra a *tutti* stand-up bow. They will
let you know if you should get one by yourself, usually by
tapping their bows on the stands or clapping. The concertmaster might gesture to you to take this one by yourself. Do
not be offended if they do not offer this. Each orchestra has
its own way of showing appreciation or lack thereof.

20. If you can, wait in the wings after the performance and
thank the individual musicians who come out on that side
of the stage. It is a nice gesture, and they appreciate the
opportunity to shake hands with the conductor. They also
want to get to the snack bar quickly.

There are so many more little bits of information to be gleaned
as you go about pursuing your career, but let no detail go unnoticed. Keep track of what works and what does not. These lessons
will be cumulative, and eventually you will develop a set of patterns
that works in almost any situation. But at the same time, conducting always brings something new. As with the music itself, there are
discoveries at every turn.

Deciding if you will stand or sit at rehearsal is a discretionary
matter. I vowed that I would always be on my feet, but then matters of the back started to creep in, and I began rehearsing from a
stool. It was once my belief that if you were vertical, it would make
the orchestra more attentive. Now I am not so sure it makes any
difference.

Here is something I have not changed my mind about: The
audience always makes its first judgment about the conductor from
the moment he or she enters the stage. Working on deportment is
helpful, perhaps with the aid of a posture coach, or at least a friend

who wants you to make a good impression. Do not overlook this important aspect of the conductor's craft.

We musicians have an expression: "The conductor should have the score in his head, and not his head in the score." Over the years, I have been doing more and more of the repertoire from memory. This is mostly based on years of experience performing works several times. Eventually, you develop a kind of body memory, just as pianists do not think about fingerings after practicing and playing pieces often.

Some people think of conductors who perform without the music on the stand as showboats. After all, most great orchestras can get through a great deal of the repertoire without really looking at the person on the podium. But I think the real plus of leaving the score at home for the performances is that you have a much better sense of communication with the players. Your eyes, unless they are closed, will always be on either the entire ensemble or a few members. However, do not attempt to do a work from memory if you have any insecurity whatsoever. The orchestra will sense this, and if something goes wrong, they will remember.

Should you use a stick or conduct with only your hands? This is a personal decision, and the answer depends on what you wish to accomplish. Great conductors have favored one technique over the other, and many have utilized both interchangeably. It is probably better to start out with a baton, just to get the feel of what it can do and how well it fits into your hand. If you tend toward angularity in your gestures, put the baguette down for a while and see if you can create a more natural flow of beat when you take it up again.

For those of you who aspire to make the podium your domain, it is important to observe conductors in rehearsal, more so than in performance. Watching both great and not-so-great maestri is an object lesson in what not to do. What do I mean by that? When everything is going along smoothly, it is pretty much impossible to figure out why. But if a passage does not proceed well, one can usually deduce what the conductor did wrong. This will seem obvious, but in your own path as a conductor, do the best you can to avoid falling into traps that you might have witnessed.

You cannot learn how to conduct from a book. Although a number of texts are available, the most they can do is give you written explanations of beat patterns, instructions on the use of the left hand, examples from select pieces of music, etc. It is like trying to teach someone how to pole vault without actually going onto the field. No one has written *Conducting for Dummies* yet, but there is *The Complete Idiot's Guide to Conducting Music.* Good luck to those of you who wish to learn in this manner.

One final piece of advice: The musicians always know the best places to eat, especially on tour. I once had the idea to write a little essay that told performers which restaurants are open after concerts in major cities. Do not confine yourself to the hotel or room service. Once in a while, be adventurous rather than relying on the tried and true. The following was something I heard in Paris, but just from the point of view of the musician on his cell phone, calling back to the States. He said, "You will never guess where I am! It's the Champs-Élysées, and I am standing right in front of a McDonald's. It is exactly like the one at home!"

2

ON ORCHESTRAL PERSONALITY

An identity would seem to be arrived at by the way in which the person faces and uses his experience.

—James Baldwin

Imagine, if you will, a lone violin sitting on a table with a bow placed at its side. One by one, six violinists come out, and each plays the same piece of music on the instrument. When all have completed the task, can you discern a difference in the sound coming from the fiddle? This is not about the interpretation but the actual sonic profile of each individual.

The more experienced and talented the violinist, the more singular the sound will be. The same test holds true with any instrument. Ask six pianists to play the same piece on the same keyboard, and you will hear six distinct tonal qualities. Of course, it can sometimes take a highly trained ear to perceive the differences, but those disparities are always there. This is what separates the great musicians from the ordinary. Having an individual personality is how we identify those whose abilities transcend all others.

This brings me to one of the great orchestral dilemmas of our time, the loss of personality that was once a hallmark of certain combinations of ensembles and their music directors. Just as with our distinguished soloists of the past, orchestras used to be identified with a specific sound. Usually it was associated with an artistic leader who had the vision to work toward that end by hiring musicians who were a good fit in terms of both technical ability and blend.

Strict attention to how a newcomer to the orchestra would match with the others supported the development of "The Stokowski/Ormandy Philadelphia Sound," "Reiner's Chicagoans," "Szell's Clevelanders," etc. These musical autocrats created a soundscape that was recognizable from the first bar of any given piece of music, regardless of style. They also had an innate understanding of the overall sound they wanted their orchestras to achieve, and they were willing to showcase the idiomatic character of the ensemble in a wide variety of repertoire.

When a guest conductor would come in, he would inherit the sound associated with that orchestra's music director unless the visiting maestro was truly a genius or musical wonder. The visitor had to walk a fine line when deciding whether or not to attempt to alter this individuality. But in a few cases, a very strong person on the podium could have a profound effect on the musicians without ever saying a word. The casual glance, flick of the baton, or gesture of the left hand might produce a distinct change in the collective sound, without anyone understanding why this occurred.

The first time I led the Philadelphians in the Academy of Music, my program included the Second Symphony by Rachmaninov, a house specialty of Eugene Ormandy. Until I arrived, the orchestra had always observed what were at that time traditional cuts. The work is long, and for reasons having to do with early recording limitations, these modifications were approved by the composer. The first half of the program contained music by American composers, not often programmed by Ormandy. Leading unfamiliar works is much easier than attempting those from the standard repertoire, at least when you are working with one of the great orchestras.

After an initial run-through of the symphony, it was fairly clear that with the exception of the newly reinstated music, the Rachmaninov was simply going to be performed in the manner that the orchestra was used to. Yes, some of my tempi were different, and there were textural and internal details that I wanted to highlight, but the overall sound of the orchestra was unchanged. I wound up comparing it to a week-long visit to someone's house. Your presence changes the dynamic of everyday life a little, but you would not move the furniture around.

The reverse can also occur, but this is much rarer. I was invited to watch the very same Ormandy make a guest-conducting appearance with the Chicago Symphony Orchestra (CSO). The major work on the program was the Third Symphony by Glière, a piece seldom encountered in the concert hall these days. After ten minutes, without saying a word, the maestro had the CSO sounding very much like his own orchestra in Philly. And when Sir Georg Solti came to St. Louis to conduct a benefit concert, it likewise took only ten minutes and no speaking from him to transform my very own orchestra into a much more tension-filled ensemble, closer in sound to his charges up north.

These same metamorphoses do not, of course, apply to our most distinguished solo instrumentalists and vocalists. In fact, we go to hear them precisely for their individuality. The collective listening conscience wants to be able to identify who is playing. Imagine if, for example, Yo-Yo Ma completely changed his own sonic presence for each work on a recital. Needless to say, interpretive matters, such as the use of vibrato or the range of dynamics, come into play. But for the most part, he will always be Yo-Yo. The same goes for Renée Fleming or any other artist with a recognizable tonal profile.

Today, we do not seem so concerned about personality when it comes to orchestral sound. Even though our instrumental and vocal soloists can put their own stamp on various pieces of music, we have arrived at a time when orchestras are beginning to sound very much alike. There are many reasons for this. Some have to do with the audition process, a subject I will tackle in a later chapter. Another factor is the homogeneity of teaching, which in many respects focuses on technique over actual sound production. And the worldwide pool of musicians, coming from many different schools of thought, contributes as well.

That last sentence is an understatement. Up until thirty years ago, seeing an Asian face in an American orchestra was a rarity. Today, our orchestras not only sound different but look different as well. We have moved from a set of European traditions, which led to an American school of performance, to an aesthetic that reflects the varied training backgrounds of today's musicians. As a result, creating a unified sonority for an orchestra has become more and more difficult. Many of the young aspirants come to conservatories from abroad to get closer to the Western approach to performance practice, leading to a compromise in sound production.

At the same time, the orchestras in Japan, Korea, and China, among other countries, are sounding more and more like their counterparts in the West. Many of the students who go to the United States or Europe for training return to their homelands and bring with them what they have learned about our musical performance culture. But many stay in America and enter the workplace. Their technical proficiency is often astonishing, and they have the stamina and acuity to handle the audition process with relative ease. Their cultures have promoted musical learning from early ages, and almost all children have this world of the arts open to them.

Contrast that with the American student, not the one in music school but the one who, from the third or fourth grade on, has an education based on preparing for a battery of tests to facilitate getting into an institution of higher learning. If that young person is preparing for a musical career, it is not until he or she gets into a conservatory or college-level music program that the rigors of competitive life in the profession really kick in.

Still, it used to be within the province of the music director to establish the auditory imagery for the entirety of the orchestra. When young musicians audition for an ensemble today, most likely they do not take into account whether or not their sound matches the ideals of the conductor. Of course, in the past, when we did not have fifty-two-week seasons, music directors spent at least half the season with their own orchestras. The ability to globe-trot and serve as the leader of more than one ensemble has taken that valuable stay-at-home time away and has limited the capacity for creating a singular sound.

On one occasion, a young harpist came to ask me about applying for the vacancy that existed in the Cleveland Orchestra. She said, "I know that they are used to someone playing in the style of Marcel Grandjany (French and mellow), but I play more like Carlos Salzedo (slightly aggressive). What should I do?"

My advice was simple. "Don't take the audition. Why would you want to change the way you play after years of study, only to throw that experience away and perform in a manner that is incompatible with your own training?"

At least she knew what the Clevelanders might be looking for, which is more than can be said of most people applying for orchestral positions. Today's landscape is quite different. I will address this in more detail in the chapters regarding diversity and auditions, but for the purposes of this topic, we must take into account the person who shapes the world of orchestral sound, the music director.

When thinking about why this international school of sonority exists today, the first reason that comes to mind is that most conductors do not focus on the totality of sound an orchestra makes across various types of repertoire. We have moved to a time when, as several have put it, "There is only the sound of the composer." Whether or not we expand that notion to the field of historically informed music practice, or even to the make of instruments that the musicians utilize, I would still argue that trying to replicate how a piece might have sounded many years ago is an exercise in frustration. We do not play by candlelight, the audience does not arrive in horse-driven carriages, and most importantly, we are influenced by the sights and sounds that are around us every day.

From my perspective, understanding what the traditions might be is significant, but maintaining a consistent audio quality is perhaps even more valuable. I remember one visit to the Czech Philharmonic when we were preparing for a performance of *Le Sacre du printemps*. At a break in the first rehearsal, some of the brass players came to me, knowing that I worked quite often at that time with the CSO.

"How can we sound more like them?" they wanted to know.

"If I wanted to have the CSO sound, then I would conduct the work there, not in Prague," I answered.

Celebrating the individual qualities of an ensemble is vital to the orchestral organism. At this point in my musical life, giving performances that are good, but similar to each other, is not enough. I want to cherish the differences when they are on a high-quality level. It makes me rethink how I approach a piece of music and, consequently, increases my appreciation for musical character. My own background puts me in what might be called the Russian American school of performance. That, coupled with a very American way of life, has shaped my ideas concerning how a piece of music should sound.

The orchestras I have led over the years have also informed my thoughts. For example, when I went to the Detroit Symphony as music director, the master string parts came from the legendary leader of the orchestra, Mischa Mischakoff. In addition to being concertmaster in Detroit, he was Toscanini's pick to head the NBC Symphony. Traditional bowings, phrasing, and articulations can be tinkered with, but it is a shame to see them lost altogether. Vestiges of what made some orchestras great may still be lurking in the libraries.

My friend Marc Gordon, former English hornist with the St. Louis Symphony Orchestra, had an interesting observation:

> When I was in school and subjected to "drop the needle tests," my professors were surprised that I would not only name the piece but what orchestra was on the recording. I could tell by the sound of the oboe. The oboists in the Philadelphia, Boston, New York, Chicago, Minneapolis (then) had very distinctive tone qualities and styles. These were very recognizable to us oboe students. Oboists who studied with these teachers would naturally be influenced by their playing and teaching concepts. As a teacher over the past few decades, I saw students who studied with a particular oboist travel to take lessons from a teacher in a different location and be influenced by the different style, tone quality and, in our case, reed-making. I suspect that over time, exposure to different influences resulted in a melding of the components that contributed to the style of a particular oboist. I find it more difficult to identify a specific school of oboe playing these days than years ago. I don't opine that this is either good or bad . . . just different. It seems logical that this could be a factor with other instrument pedagogy as well, which could be a contributing factor to the issue discussed about orchestral sound and style.[1]

My experiences with ensembles in England, France, and Germany broadened my understanding of certain sonic traditions. For example, whenever I do the French repertoire with my former orchestra in Lyon, I know that in particular, the woodwinds will be playing on instruments primarily made according to the practice that originated in that country. This gives them an unusually light and at the same time slightly clearer sound than other practitioners in different countries. When I come to do the same repertoire in other regions, I do not ask the instrumentalists to change the instrument they are playing on. Today, musicians tend to select models that suit their individual needs and not the collective sound.

Individuality does come at a price and is sometimes exaggerated. These days, a few performers are opting to play exactly what they see on the page, with little or no variation from the printed text. In the Mendelssohn Violin Concerto, for example, it is a long-established tradition to slow down when the second theme arrives. I have been on the podium when some soloists have insisted on maintaining the tempo that was established at the start of the work. It is not what I prefer, but certainly the violinist has the last word.

In contrast, some musicians seem to be going to the opposite extreme by presenting works in an exaggerated manner or with visual accompaniments that distract the listener from the music. One can certainly point to artists from the past who opposed the norms in order to be individual. Notably, Leopold Stokowski and Glenn Gould often strayed from the usual path, but they always had a substantive answer when asked why they made the interpretive decisions they did. Some artists might simply say, "I feel the music this way." That is not enough. Artistic choices must be substantiated by true musical reasons.

The conclusion is simple: The conductor, soloist, and orchestra, as products of their own time, must find a balanced approach to interpretation, one that represents both the wishes of the composer and themselves. Give composers the chance to shine in the light that exists in this century, but do not give in to the one-size-fits-all category. Make your ensemble sound like none other than yours and the composer's.

3

ON SIZE

I like those older theaters—the acoustics are perfect, I
mean, you just have that feel of there's been a thousand
shows in there and now you get to be one.

—Billy Gardell

To step foot in a grand opera house, concert hall, museum, or old
movie palace for the first time is one of the great experiences of
childhood. The audible gasps and expressions of "wow," "amazing,"
or "cool" that permeate the big spaces encapsulate the very meaning
of the artistic experience. Most of those kids don't think about the
sound. For them, it is an entrance into a visual world that cannot be
duplicated on the big screen or even in a painting. They have never
seen anything like it before.

Musicians see it in another way. When they sing their first
words, play their first notes, or simply imagine what the place might
sound like, the aural properties of the hall can shape their next few
moments, or even their lives. Most people can discern good acoustics versus poor ones, but the majority do not know why something
sounds the way it does. Even musicians, supposedly used to telling
the difference, cannot accurately say why one venue is superior to
another.

What some musicians do say is that in order to maintain a
"world-class reputation," the size of the orchestra as well as the
number of weeks they play during a season are what matters. The

gulf between the desired orchestra complement and what is necessary to fill the hall with sound is quite wide and often completely misunderstood by the public.

But let's start with the acoustics. Just as the pianist has a Steinway, the violinist a Stradivarius, or the cymbal player a Zildjian, the orchestra has its hall. In fact, the facility in which the ensemble performs is the instrument of the group. You can put the finest equipment in the greatest musicians' hands, but if the hall is dry, their sound will be dry as well. On the other hand, too much reverberance results in a murky sound and a lack of clarity. All musicians will agree that the acoustics of a great hall must be balanced between the two extremes.

Whenever I come to a theater in which I have never performed, I run a simple test prior to the first rehearsal—I stand in the middle of the stage and clap once. If the sound reverberates for a bit more than one second, that means the acoustics are about right. After that, when I begin conducting, my focus is on not only the music but also whether the musicians can hear each other. This is especially important for the back desks of strings. Assuming that the first violins are on the left and the cellos on the right, my question is this: can the players at the extreme ends hear across the stage?

Usually the answer is no, but if there is enough clarity on the platform, most of what is being played can be discerned. Sometimes the winds and percussion are on risers, placing them a bit higher than the string section. This can help with listening onstage but often results in an overbalance in favor of those who are seated above their colleagues. It is always helpful to have a pair of ears in the hall during rehearsals to assist in attaining proper balances.

However, this may not solve certain issues that can only be detected during performance. An audience has a role to play, not just as listeners but also as a physical presence that can alter the listening experience in the hall. Bodies absorb sound, just as the material on the seats does. The science of acoustics is imprecise due to such variables, making it difficult to predict what the situation will be like on a given day. I have sat in many a concert hall for the first half of a program and then moved around after intermission. Even being just a few seats away can change what one hears.

In olden times, most opera houses and the few concert venues that existed were smaller than those of today. I remember being quite surprised when attending a performance of *Don Giovanni* in Prague, at the Estates Theatre where the work was premiered. The building only seats 650, and the intimacy this brings to operas performed there is astonishing. In fact, most opera houses in Europe tend to be on the smaller side. The grand palaces would come later, bringing with them greater challenges for everyone, especially the singers.

In their excellent treatise entitled *The Idiomatic Orchestra*, authors Karl Aage Rasmussen and Lasse Laursen provide this interesting piece of information:

> In 1782, the permanent staff of the Mannheim Orchestra included 23 violins (12/11), 3 violas, 4 cellos, 3 double basses, 4 flutes, 3 oboes, 4 clarinets, 4 bassoons, 6 horns, and kettledrums. Around 1800, the string group had grown to 7 violas, 5 cellos and 7 double basses, and from here on the size of the string section was repeatedly extended.

They go on to write:

> The financial slowdown after the First World War and the worldwide Depression during the 1930s led to a decrease in orchestral size, and since the Second World War the orchestra has essentially stalled at the relative size at which we find it today. But even today, orchestral forces vary considerably due to a number of conditions: economy, the size of the stage or hall, function (for instance opera), score requirements, acoustics, repertoire, the conductor's special wishes, local traditions, etc.[1]

So often the artistic decision is not just a matter of what the composer might have wanted but also a result of the conditions of the time. Berlioz seems to have been the first one to truly expand the orchestra, but by his time, there were actual conductors, not continuo players. When Strauss or Mahler wrote their huge compositions, it was because they had these orchestral forces at their disposal. But what about the poor singers who had to make almost impossible transitions?

Imagine being trained in one of the little jewels and then suddenly being thrust into the Metropolitan or Covent Garden houses, with five times the number of seats. No wonder there are talks about discreet amplification, possibly preserving a singer's voice for a few more years. But that is what grand opera seems to be about. Bigger is better, and a lot of great works require the large-scale palazzos.

It is important to keep in mind that the demand for entertainment was determined by what existed at the time. Operas not only catered to the rich but, especially in Italy, were also a part of every community's experience. With no radio, television, or internet, works for the stage became an increasingly popular way for audiences to be entertained and moved by the combination of word and drama. Similarly, music in the household was common, with most homes filled with songs accompanied by piano or other instruments.

Time rolled on, and the public found other distractions. Today, the competition in the entertainment world—and do not be fooled, concerts and opera are entertainment—causes artistic institutions to reconsider which comes first, the art or the customer. Almost everyone will tell you that the majority of performing institutions are suffering because of an ability to attract a large enough audience to fill the hall. The old methods of subscription schemes, various ticket pricing systems, and even less-than-subtle marketing ploys may work in the short run, but sustaining that model into the future seems like an impossible task.

There is nothing quite so discouraging as walking onto the stage and seeing almost half the seats unfilled. We try to do our best to make great music for those who have come to the concert, but lurking in the background is the overwhelming fear that the next performance might see a further decline in attendance. In the United States, only 30 percent or so of revenue comes from ticket sales. The rest of the budget relies solely on the generosity of individuals, foundations, or corporations, mostly representing a generation that understood the full value of a thriving cultural community.

So how many musicians do you think are required to put on a concert? It depends on two things: the repertoire and, at least to me, the size of the hall. Sometimes these go hand in hand. Many composers specify the number of instrumentalists needed to play their work. Others leave it to the performers. When I went to Detroit, the orchestra was actually larger than it is as of this writing. Following a six-month work stoppage in 2010–2011, the organization reduced the number of musicians from ninety-six to eighty-five, but this roster was sufficient for performing the majority of the repertoire. The music itself did not suffer. Why not? Because the hall is relatively small in comparison to many other venues in the United States.

When we played very large-scale works, we hired extra musicians to make up any difference between the standard complement and what the music required. This core contingent has grown by a few musicians over the years as the orchestra's financial picture has improved. With some very creative devices, including free webcasts and community engagement initiatives aimed at increasing accessibility, we were able to boost our attendance significantly, and when donors see good-sized audiences week to week, they tend to make larger and more frequent contributions. But it's important to note that because of the size of the hall, we did not need to have as many full-time musicians as some other orchestras.

Okay Slatkin. Under your premise, a larger venue should therefore have a bigger orchestra? Not necessarily. In most music written prior to the 20th century, having too many musicians onstage, no matter how large the venue, creates an unwieldy sound, inappropriate for the piece being performed. And again, we have to take into account the sonic perception from the audience's point of view.

Some halls fully project sound to the listener, while others, sadly, retain most of the good stuff on the stage. Perhaps you have heard that sitting in the upper reaches of the balcony is the best place to experience a concert. That is correct. Sound rises, and its projection is paramount in any auditorium or opera house. If possible, one should avoid sitting in those seats that are underneath a balcony or overhang. They may be the most expensive, but they provide the least auditory satisfaction.

Is there an ideal size in terms of the number of musicians employed by the orchestra's management? This is a very tricky question, as it brings into play years of collective-bargaining history with individual orchestras. As of this writing, the largest ensemble in the United States comprises 106 musicians. Do all of them play at once? Not very often.

If you want answers, you will have to look at the various agreements made by each group. The rules and regulations found in these documents make congressional bills seem like children's books. They stipulate how much time off musicians have, even within a given concert, as well as the number of weeks individual musicians play. Indeed, orchestral musicians have won many hard-fought battles through collective bargaining. There was a time, not so long ago, when being a member of the orchestra was a part-time job. Don't get me wrong. I strongly support each musician earning as much as possible for a skill that is exhibited by only a few.

Today, being employed by a cultural institution, as a musician or an executive, can be highly lucrative. However, over the past ten years or so, we have begun to see cracks in the financial wall. In this supply-and-demand culture, defending the fees paid is becoming more and more difficult. For example, a glance at the program book might reveal a roster of ninety-two musicians, but in the case of a concert featuring Mozart, perhaps only forty musicians are required. How do you explain to the average concertgoer what all of the other full-time members of the orchestra are doing that week?

As mentioned earlier, acoustics is an inexact science, at least as far as the concert hall or opera house is concerned. The orchestra complement that seems excellent for one environment might be awful for another. Think of it like your sound system at home. If you are an audiophile, you will tinker almost endlessly to get it to your own liking. We cannot do that with the orchestra. Nonetheless, it is possible to move the musicians around, trying to figure out what works best for the facility.

In St. Louis, the cellos sat on the outside right of the stage. This worked well for the spacious capacity of the hall as well as the generous reverberation time. For the National Symphony, which suffered from the poor acoustics of the original incarnation of the Kennedy Center concert hall, we eventually settled on putting the second violins on the outside right and moving the cellos and basses to the position formerly occupied by the seconds. This setup mirrored an older model of orchestra seating from the opera house tradition. Positioning the double basses on the left helped address the hall's deficiency in projecting sounds on the low end of the spectrum. The current music director has since moved the first and second violin sections back together.

In Detroit, where the cellos were on the right, I had them trade places with the violas. The hall is great, but I was looking for more definition from the alto instruments and better projection of the cellos into the hall as opposed to across the stage.

Any number of seating variations exist for the wind and percussion instruments. Leopold Stokowski even tried placing the woodwinds at the front of the ensemble. Some conductors are experimenting with individual musicians scattered throughout the orchestra in different positions than they normally occupy, although any rearrangement raises questions about how well these players hear each other, not to mention the audience perception from different points in the hall.

Size does matter, but it is all proportional to the space in which the orchestra plays. We want to foster that awe that comes from the child who sees the hall for the first time, but eventually, we want that attention to turn to the world of sound, perhaps eliciting not only wonder, but also inspiration.

4

ON THE THEATER

Music of all arts should be expansive and inclusive.

—Jesse Jackson

A few years ago, I had the pleasure of dining with Riccardo Muti after a concert I conducted with the ONL (Orchestre National de Lyon) at the Ravenna Festival. It was a most pleasant evening, one that stretched into the morning hours. The maestro had much to say, and we had never really conversed prior to this night.

At one point, he asked me a very direct question: "You are not a man of the theater; are you?"

I explained that opera was really not part of my experience as a young person, and my passions leaned more toward orchestral, jazz, and chamber music. After that, I went on to speak of my family background in music and living in a household filled with vastly different styles of music, excluding opera. At the time, Los Angeles did not have its own company, and the San Francisco Opera came down south for only a couple performances each year.

While I was familiar with the repertoire via recordings and broadcast performances, opera was outside my comfort zone when I began my career. Although my principal conducting teachers were both schooled in the pit, they rarely taught their students much about this side of the repertoire, much less the differences between leading orchestras on and below the stage.

I was reminded of the Muti query when I read that the recently deceased Mariss Jansons's father, Arvīds, had said that conductors

31

should begin their musical training in the opera house. Although his son had done very little in that department, there certainly was a time when many aspiring conductors did, in fact, get their early experience in opera. It's also interesting to note that most European concert orchestras originated as opera house orchestras. It was not so long ago that the orchestra of the Metropolitan Opera began to give stand-alone performances at Carnegie Hall. To this day, some people do not realize that the Vienna Philharmonic is made up of musicians from the Staatsoper.

As we stumble our way through this first quarter of the 21st century, there are more outlets for conductors. Many of these opportunities were available years ago but were not really thought of as part of the standard path for those aspiring to lead orchestras. When we speak of the theater, in terms of music, rarely do ballet, musical theater, and cinema leap to mind. And yet, these are becoming more and more a part of the conductor's domain.

If we take into account pop, jazz, and choral literature, there is simply too much music and too many genres for one person to master. A few have tried, but it tends to come down to finding a degree of comfort within just a few idioms. In my own experience, I have found that conducting for the ballet is the most difficult of all. Tempos are hard to judge, costumes sometimes make it impossible to tell whom to follow, and some of the orchestral music is quite complicated.

One of my teachers, Jean Morel, when asked about the difference between conducting opera and ballet, had a truly great answer: "They are the same, except that when the dancer comes to the top, she must come down." Of course, it is more complex than that, but it is clear what he meant. Simultaneously coordinating what is happening onstage with the music in the pit is only one of the conductor's responsibilities. Putting disparate elements together so they flow seamlessly takes great concentration and genuine musical skill.

But is that any different for the other above-mentioned genres? Not really. Take film, for example. Now here is an art that used to be dismissed as inferior to virtually every other. Never mind that in the past, almost all composers for cinema were classically trained and educated. In 1908 Camille Saint-Saëns became the first prominent composer of a film score, signaling the emergence of the new form as a pathway to the future for those who had previously written for opera and ballet.

Whether it was George Gershwin, Dmitri Shostakovich, Leonard Bernstein, Aaron Copland, Miklós Rózsa, or Nino Rota, the film bandwagon was something that many composers jumped on. Some succeeded to the point that they shed their allegiance to the traditional forms of writing, concentrating entirely on the silver screen. For a few, this was clearly a way to earn significantly more money. For others, it was a way to escape the horrors of World War II. If the first quarter of the 20th century saw New York as the musical capital of the United States, there was a gradual shift to Los Angeles as the decades moved forward, although the East Coast still remained the destination for many artists.

In order for a motion picture to be coordinated with the music, an entirely different way of conducting was required, at first just following what was on the screen and hoping for the best. Streamers, timecodes, punches, and click tracks took the musicians into the next phase. And, beginning at the turn of the 21st century, presenting entire film scores became commonplace in the concert hall. But not every conductor is equipped or trained to do this.

Many scores for silent films, and even contemporary ones, require conductors to lead the orchestra for a good hour and a half with no pause, almost the length of *Salome*. Since there is no give and take, conductors have to put their own musical instincts on pause and make sure that the beat is synchronized exactly to the picture. Any interpretive choices must fit within the parameters dictated by the visuals, and we must be mindful not to make the music more important than the film. The really fine performances, few and far between, are those in which the conductor and orchestra not only hit all the marks but also bring forward their finest musicianship to amplify what is happening on the screen.

Just listen to some of the great film music in its original form from the 1940s and 1950s. All eleven studio orchestras in the States were incredible, easily outclassing most of the ensembles playing symphonic repertoire, and each had its own, distinctive sound. With my father as concertmaster at 20th Century Fox and my mom as first cellist at Warner Brothers, I ear-witnessed the quality and individuality of these ensembles time and time again. The difference in sound that these two orchestras created was instantly recognizable. The same held true for MGM, Paramount, and all the others.

John Williams once told me that the most difficult form of composition for the screen was the cartoon. The music has to be even more precise, and delivered in a shorter timeframe, than the usual motion picture. That is why he has never written for Bugs Bunny. Go back and listen to, and watch, any animation from the same period as the Golden Age of Hollywood to hear the most astonishing music played with remarkable precision and musicianship.

Since the early days of sound, filmmakers have used classical music as a background effect or for thematic emphasis in a given scene. I find most references to classical music in film a bit annoying unless they move the plot along or add something to the visual impact. The reason is simple: I wind up concentrating on the wrong thing. Maybe that is just because I am a musician who recognizes the piece. However, some composers manage to cleverly interweave fragments of either their own scores, or the music of others, into the framework of the film.

At this point you might be asking, "What does this have to do with being a man of the theater?" Well, when I was a youngster, we did not go to multiplexes or cinematheques. We went to the movie theater. Conducting this music in the proper manner and style was something that came as naturally to me as opera conducting did for others. Not only were my parents involved in the music end of the film industry, they were also mainstays of Capitol Records in both the popular and classical divisions. Being surrounded by the greats in the pop and jazz world prepared me for some of my first conducting experiences when I began as assistant conductor in St. Louis.

In 1971 I gave the world premiere of a live version of *Jesus Christ Superstar*, which began its life as a two-record rock opera. It brought a much different audience into the concert hall. Prior to the 1970s, pops concerts were given more in the manner of Arthur Fiedler and the Boston Pops Orchestra. His unique format was simple and elegant. The program was often divided into three sets: first, a selection of short, classical favorites; next, an equally popular concerto; and finally, arrangements of music from the stage, screen, and pop charts. After all, it was only natural that recording artists would want to promote their songs, and one way to do that was via the concert hall.

With radio starting to decline and television becoming the medium of choice for getting one's musical message out, a few individuals and acts had orchestrations made of their best-selling tunes. The Boston Pops would play them, and then they would be broadcast on TV. It was a tremendously effective marketing tool. Those who could not go to the live concert could at least see some of their favorite stars perform with a live orchestra.

Just as with film, a new set of conducting techniques was needed. Often, a full score was not available, only a piano reduction with indications for a few instrumental cues once in a while. If it was a pop song or jazz chart, the words might not be included, and chords might be notated with symbols rather than the notes themselves. Conductors not versed in this shorthand found themselves at a loss, unless they really remembered those lessons in harmony and theory. Even then, the classical training simply did not prepare them for all the discrepancies between the score and the parts.

These early variants of crossover music were difficult for many. Surprisingly, a number of the most renowned singers did not read music, relying on their basic musicality and vocal training. How was the conductor supposed to communicate with them if the usual point of reference, the printed musical text, was incoherent for one party? Again, I grew up knowing many of these artists, so it was second nature to me. If something was not going correctly, you just sang or pointed out the lyric, then said, "I will cue you in." Seems simple enough, but surprisingly few conductors really understood how to do this.

Then there is the world of Broadway itself. Born out of the operetta, moved forward by Rudolf Friml, Victor Herbert, and Gilbert and Sullivan, among others, musical theater evolved as a particularly American medium. By the time we got to Rodgers and Hammerstein (or Lorenz Hart), Lerner and Loewe, George and Ira Gershwin, Cole Porter, and Stephen Sondheim, it was clear that something new was in the air. I have always found it amusing that the name of the lyricist is credited alongside the composer for the vast majority of works for Broadway, but the name of the librettist for an opera is never included in the same way.

> Broadway has changed tremendously from the early days when the shows were referred to as musical comedies. Musical Theater is now a more expanded art form. Back then, singer/actors were not the norm. From the 60's to now, it is necessary to do it all to be a consummate Broadway performer.
>
> —Betty Buckley

I, for one, never thought of *Carousel, My Fair Lady,* or *West Side Story* as musical comedies, but I understand what the great lady was talking about. Having led all three of these shows, I can say that they are just as difficult and complex as any work written for the combination of stage and pit. Add to that the stylistic differences between them, and it is impossible for me to make a case that musical theater is a lesser form of art than any of the others that grace the stage.

As I glance at the list of music directors leading major orchestras around the world today, I notice that very few of them started their musical lives in the pit. They may have known the repertoire at an early age, but the opportunities in the operatic world were decreasing while those in the orchestral sector were increasing. From around the 1920s on, more works written for instrumental ensembles were entering the repertoire while, for the most part, stage pieces were few and far between. Apprenticeships for conductors with symphony orchestras were plentiful from the 1950s onward, but unless you were a répétiteur (rehearsal pianist), there were fewer chances to work with an opera company.

These days, the majority of conductors move back and forth between the concert hall and the pit. Many put on un-staged or semi-staged performances of the great works from the opera house. This concept presents several problems, not the least of which is managing the balance between voices and instruments, but it has been something passed down from the time of Toscanini and even before. My mother used to tell of being dragged to a concert version of *Lohengrin*—all of it—and thereafter swearing that she would never step foot in an opera house.

As for me, I have enjoyed most of my experiences in the pit. Unfortunately, there are usually compromises, sometimes with a member or two of the cast, sometimes with the production team, and sometimes because I do not love every note of the score.

This quote, attributed to Rossini, sums up a few of my thoughts about certain stage works: "Wagner's operas contain wonderful moments but terrible half hours." I wouldn't go quite that far, and there are certainly works in the symphonic canon that contain some padding, but I believe that it comes down to understanding something more basic. Obviously works that include an additional element, whether opera, ballet, film, or song, tell some kind of story. Most orchestral, chamber, and solo pieces do not. It is a question of concrete versus abstract. One conveys the vision to the person listening or viewing, and the other allows that person to create, or not, what a given piece of music might represent.

Music is one of the arts that has a middleman. In a museum, there is a direct connection between the artist and the person looking at the painting or sculpture. The performing arts, on the other hand, place the interpreters somewhere in between the creator and the listener or viewer. It does not matter if it is a live performance or a recording. It is our job to imagine what it is that the creators had in their minds and souls when we attempt to fulfill their vision. If we do not, then we have failed in terms of our duties to both the originator of the idea and the people who listen and observe.

5

ON NATIONALISM

Every day at some point I encounter some sort of anti-American feeling.

—Chelsea Clinton

Atlanta, Baltimore, Boston, Chicago, Cincinnati, Cleveland, Dallas, Detroit, Houston, Indianapolis, Los Angeles, Minnesota, New York, Philadelphia, Pittsburgh, San Diego, San Francisco, Seattle, St. Louis, Washington, DC.

What do these twenty orchestras have in common?

Eighteen of them currently have music directors who were neither born nor trained in the United States. The two with Americans at the helm as of this writing are in a search for their next artistic leader. Barring some surprise, more than likely, these posts will also go to conductors from abroad. We are speaking of the highest-paying orchestras in the land, at least as far as musician salaries are concerned.

It was not so long ago that Michael Tilson Thomas, Gerard Schwarz, David Robertson, Robert Spano, Marin Alsop, and I, all American-born, served as music director of one of these ensembles during the same period of time. On top of that, all of us were very active on the guest conducting scene, along with several of our colleagues. Somebody must have had enough faith to engage each of us time and time again.

No, this is not going to be a diatribe against anyone leading an orchestra now. It is not going to be an anti-board rant. It is not going to be a rehashing of xenophobic rhetoric. What it will be is an examination of what this country might be doing wrong in the 21st century. In order to do that, we have to go back a bit.

In 1845, the ten-year-old Theodore Thomas arrived in New York from Esens, Germany. His father was a band master and violinist, and the young man took up the instrument at an early age. He founded the Theodore Thomas Orchestra in 1862. He was named music director of the New York Philharmonic in 1877 for one season and returned for two additional seasons in 1879.

During a meeting in New York, a businessman and supporter of the Thomas orchestra asked the maestro if he would be interested in coming to Chicago and forming a symphony for that city. He famously replied, "I would go to hell if they gave me a permanent orchestra." On October 16, 1891, the first concert by the Chicago Orchestra was given at Auditorium Theatre. Upon the maestro's unexpected death in 1905, the name of the ensemble was changed to the Theodore Thomas Orchestra before eventually being renamed the Chicago Symphony Orchestra. In his lifetime, Thomas was unparalleled in his contributions to the musical life of this country and the growth of the American symphony orchestra.

It would take more than fifty years for a "Big Five" US orchestra to name one of its own countrymen as music director. In 1958, Leonard Bernstein was appointed to the New York Philharmonic, although there had been some discussion of him taking over in Boston a few years earlier. A few natives had led other groups over the years, but now, for the first time, a major American-born and American-trained conductor headed up one of the nation's most prestigious ensembles.

What makes this particularly interesting is that foreign-born musicians introduced to this country the vast majority of what we might call the classics of American repertoire. In particular, world premieres of works by Copland, Harris, Schuman, Piston, Sessions, and Grofé were led by Koussevitzky, Reiner, Stokowski, Ormandy, Mitropoulos, and Toscanini. These conductors were the standard-bearers for the works that became hallmarks of symphonic tradition in the United States.

It is also important to remember that many members of the orchestras, especially the principal players, were likewise born abroad. The NBC Symphony and Philadelphia Orchestra were populated with Italians, while the Boston Symphony had its French and German contingents. American instrumental students were learning their craft from these old-world instructors. Gradually more native-born pedagogues began to teach in our conservatories, and the result was a uniquely American sound that evolved out of the various styles that had been taught previously.

The same was true of the conductors following in the footsteps of Bernstein. Lenny was a master of all genres, whether classical, jazz, pop, or Broadway. Unlike the majority of his European counterparts, he was comfortable switching conducting roles in the same way he could change styles as a composer. This would become typical of American conductors and was also a hallmark of several American composers.

Aaron Copland, for example, was using jazz elements in his very early works, and William Schuman was a song peddler in Tin Pan Alley. Morton Gould was a composer for radio shows. Roy Harris tapped into the populist folklore, as did Virgil Thomson. During the Fifties, television was starting to play a more important role in the lives of everyday Americans. It presented a new avenue for conductors to explore, and naturally, Bernstein took advantage of this. The concept of verbal communication with an audience was rare until that time.

What lay beneath the reticence of boards to select Americans to lead their orchestras?

For most of the time up until the mid-1960s, the musicians had little say over who would direct them. These decisions came from people in social and business circles, many of whom did not have a great deal of musical knowledge. Taking their cues from a few industry leaders, they relied on their own conceptions of not only what a music director should do but also how he (always a "he") should look and speak. The exoticism of another accent was most appealing.

Table 5.1.

1911	San Francisco Symphony	Henry Hadley
1911	Dallas Symphony	Walter Fried
1914	Detroit Symphony	Weston Gales
1926	Seattle Symphony	Karl Krueger
1930	Baltimore Symphony	George Siemonn
1936	Houston Symphony	Ernst Hoffmann
1943	Los Angeles Philharmonic	Alfred Wallenstein
1945	Atlanta Symphony	Henry Sopkin
1947	Cincinnati Symphony	Thor Johnson
1949	National Symphony	Howard Mitchell
1953	San Diego Symphony	Robert Shaw
1956	Indianapolis Symphony	Izler Solomon
1958	New York Philharmonic	Leonard Bernstein
1972	Cleveland Orchestra	Lorin Maazel*
1979	St. Louis Symphony	Leonard Slatkin
1984	Pittsburgh Symphony	Lorin Maazel
2004	Boston Symphony	James Levine

*born in France to American parents

After all, a European conductor would most certainly have a greater understanding of the standard repertoire!

Bernstein paved the way, but not just because he was "America's Conductor." With acclaim from abroad, he also had an international appeal that was previously unheard of for someone brought up entirely in the States. Composers had gone to Europe to study, particularly with Nadia Boulanger in Paris. When they concluded their time with her, she told them to "Go home and create American music for the concert hall." They followed her advice.

It took a little time for other orchestras to put prominent conductors from the USA into the top slots. Here are some examples of the first homegrown talents that made it. They are taken from the twenty that I began the chapter discussing (see table 5.1).

As of this writing, the Philadelphia Orchestra, the Minnesota Orchestra, and the Chicago Symphony Orchestra have never had an American-born music director.

What does this information from the past tell us about the future?

First and foremost is that we have not set up adequate training for our budding artistic leaders. I personally feel that actual lessons are not that crucial, as leading an orchestra is something that you learn by doing. Many of the great conductors in the past had what we would consider today poor technique. But they knew what they wanted and how to get it during rehearsals.

The leading country for learning podium behavior appears to be Finland. Jorma Panula has become legendary for his classes, and he is turning out fine leaders who conduct orchestras all over the world. We do not have anything like that here. The reason is simple, in my opinion. Most of the conductors who are associated with conservatories are also active as either guest conductors or even music directors. They do not have the time to spend full years with their students.

My own teacher, Jean Morel, realized that he was not going to make it to the big time. Instead, somewhat bitterly I think, he devoted himself to The Juilliard School, just as Panula has done in Helsinki. It amuses me when I am handed a CV of a young conductor to see that they list me among their teachers. In reality, most of them may have been part of just one master class I gave. There has never been a point in my life when I have taught conducting for more than two weeks at a time.

When I relinquished my music director positions, more time was freed up for education. Rather than work exclusively at one school, I divided my time among two or three. In each instance, the students had been selected by others, so I did not have input as to who was participating. Perhaps it is time to create a curriculum for the modern American conductor, one that can be implemented with a school and a professional symphony orchestra. It does little good to teach violin without the physical instrument available to the student. It is the same for the conductor with an ensemble. And having the resource of musicians who have performed the repertoire many times might attract a highly skilled level of young prospects.

Working with an orchestra, and at least on a regular basis with its music director, is critical in developing the next generation of artistic leaders. In Washington, for nine seasons, we ran the National Conducting Institute, where four aspiring maestri worked with the orchestra, management, and staff, as well as with me. It was the only program in the world in which student conductors could work with a professional orchestra. They learned just about everything you need to know regarding how an orchestra operates. In my first book, *Conducting Business,* I discuss this important initiative in detail.

Mentorship is more than just teaching. It is guiding students, and even young professionals, through the minefield of professional traps that lies ahead. For Americans, it has never been easy. We have to think of ways to get our message out there. With all the different outlets these days, you would think it would be simple.

The second possible path is to look back at those Americans who succeeded. Each of them found a niche with an emphasis on a particular part of the repertoire that was a little different from what anyone else was conducting. They championed composers who had fallen out of favor, were new and interesting, or were unknown. As usual, Bernstein covered all three bases.

But look at Shaw, with his emphasis on choral works; Previn taking on Korngold, Goldmark, and Shapero; Tilson Thomas and his mavericks; or Schippers and the American romantics. Now look at what the younger generation of today is interested in—more Mahler, Bruckner, some contemporary works, and the occasional performance of music by women or African American composers. This is fine, but what I do not see is a true individual voice, one that associates a conductor with a certain part of the repertoire.

The third problem area is within the professional ranks of the orchestras themselves. When I began as assistant conductor in St. Louis in 1968, these positions abounded. Some orchestras even had two or three junior baton-wavers watching every rehearsal, leading children's concerts, and conferring with not only the music director but every guest artist as well. Today we have "cover conductors"—those who are brought in on a week-by-week basis. They rarely do anything other than sit and listen, and I have to believe that it actually costs more for the organization.

Here is one suggestion. The era of the great American symphonists has long passed. No more Harris, Schuman, Piston, Sessions, Diamond, Mennin, Persichetti, and others. In addition, the succeeding generation has also seemingly disappeared from our concert repertoire, although their works were prominent during their lifetimes. Druckman, Erb, Crumb (who is still around), Wuorinen, et al., have simply vanished. Perhaps some enterprising conductors can find those works that draw their interest and incorporate them into an individualized repertoire.

There just might be a market for that, and young talent can make a splash by resurrecting some of these masterpieces. And one does not have to be American to do it. It makes no difference where a conductor, or any other musician, comes from. As long as you have the passion to actively promote works that mean something to you, nationality means nothing.

Still, it is my hope that the future will see more people from this country on our own podiums. With an ever-increasing number of musicians calling America their home, there is no reason to think that this cannot happen.

Facebook commentator Walter Tomaszewski noted:

> The great 19th-century Russian writer and actor Anton Chek-hov once wrote, "the best writers, or at least, the ones who in-toxicate you, are the ones who are going somewhere and beckon you to follow." I would say that the same holds true for any artist, and this includes conductors. They take you through a musical landscape (unfamiliar or well-worn), point out this, highlight that, and at journey's end thank you for being company on the trip. To me, it doesn't matter who does the leading/conducting. Every conductor will approach a work from a different point of view; that keeps any work, especially the ones that get a lot of play, fresh and exciting. It's the trip, not the destination that's im-portant. Whoever is acting as tour guide, no matter from where, will always have something new and exciting to say.[1]

The critical two words from Chekhov are "best writers." Any art form is subjective, but I don't believe that we can say that "everyone will approach a work from a different point of view." The bottom line is that regardless of where someone is from, they must have something to say as an individual. Knowing what is right for a com-munity is a prime function of a music director. That is where native talent can play a huge role now.

II

SECOND MOVEMENT

6

ON AGENTS

Music is spiritual. The music business is not.

—Claudio Monteverdi

After "What is your favorite piece of music?" the question I most dislike is, "How can I get an agent?" Many young people who ask this have no idea what a manager does, how much money representatives take from the artist, and, in several situations, how little they actually do.

Let's start with working definitions of "manager" and "agent" because there can be significant differences between them in some sectors of the industry. Within the popular music realm, for example, the agent handles booking and servicing contracts while the manager focuses on overall career strategy and goals, and each charges commission separately. In the classical music arena, however, the role of the artist manager encompasses both of these responsibilities. Depending on the size of the agency, the office of the artist manager may comprise a senior-level executive who leads the team representing the artist, a mid-level manager who acts as the primary go-between, negotiating with the presenters that hire the artist, and an associate manager who handles logistical details.

My own career, spanning almost fifty-five years now, saw me with three different management companies in the United States, way too many to remember in Europe, and three in Asia. Since I have spent most of my musical life in America, it is probably best for me to recount how it all began and where it is today.

49

There was no one to help me out during my assistantship in St. Louis. Like so many young musicians, I focused on the present and very rarely thought about what came next. On a road trip to New York with the orchestra, my teacher and mentor, Walter Susskind, suggested that we go see the most powerful man in the classical music business at the time, Ronald Wilford.

At the palace of Columbia Artists Management Incorporated (CAMI) on 57th Street, Wilford was the king. The company had more musicians under its wing than any other agency, with Wilford handling the conductor division. He followed in the footsteps of others who could move their maestri around like pawns on a chessboard. Whether Arthur Judson or Sol Hurok, these people could barter one conductor in trade for another, in some cases giving orchestras little to no choice regarding who their next music director might be.

Susskind thought that Wilford could jolt me right to the top of the heap. At that point, the hope was that Wilford would see value in signing me before anyone else snapped me up. We went to his office, and after pleasantries were exchanged, I was told that the CAMI conductor roster was full and that he would keep me in mind for the future. In other words, no dice.

I was not disappointed. Having seen how quickly young musicians could fall from grace in the profession, I felt it prudent to acquire additional experience before making another attempt at management. More than likely, had I been accepted, either my agent would have been someone less experienced anyway and I would have been just another conductor on the roster, or I would have been forced onto a faster track than I would have wanted. Biding my time seemed the best option.

This New York visit occurred in 1969, just one year into my twenty-seven-year run with the St. Louisans. At the same time, I had started to travel up to Chicago, mostly to hear concerts with that city's great orchestra and, in particular, to visit Maestro Carlo Maria Giulini. I had also established a relationship with the orchestra's executive director, John Edwards. He would become my guardian angel, acting as an advisor to orchestras and artist representatives on my behalf.

In January 1970, I led a subscription concert at home. In the audience, at the invitation of John, was Mariedi Anders, a most-respected agent from San Francisco. She broke the mold by not being part of the Big Apple group of managers, and her roster was filled with some very talented musicians, few of whom had really ascended to the top tier. After the performance she asked me to join her list, and John approved. He wanted me to start guest conducting with smaller orchestras before tackling the well-known ensembles.

This approach worked well, as I traveled to work with groups in Kansas, Oklahoma, and Oregon, as well as other good, but under-the-radar, orchestras. There was much to be learned, and I asked a lot of questions. Several of these institutions extended music-director offers, but John had other plans and would not let me take those positions. By 1974, I had jumped in for ailing conductors in New York, Chicago, and London. This catapulted my career, but the six years I spent in the trenches had prepared me, at least repertoire-wise, for the next step.

Mariedi had done the work of the representative, but John had become the de facto manager. If I could offer a piece of advice to many of my younger colleagues, it would be to find someone outside of the companies that handle a stable of artists to provide career counseling. This person needs to be familiar with the workings of the music industry, someone who can really help shape your thoughts by taking into account what you want while also understanding what is actually possible.

A few years later, there was financial trouble with Mariedi's company, causing several of her artists, including me, quite a bit in back taxes. By this time, I had developed relationships with some influential soloists and conductors. Isaac Stern wanted me to meet with his own representative, Sheldon Gold of ICM Artists Ltd., who had at one time worked under the aforementioned Wilford. If I was going to make a change, the time was now. Shelly reminded me that the purpose of an artist manager is to make money for the agency—and the better I did, the better off his organization would be.

ICM certainly boasted a lot of talent, but at this time, I was also undertaking a busy conducting life in Europe. Harold Holt Ltd. in London represented me as a regional manager; however, each country also had a local management company with its own slice of the commission pie. For instance, if I had a concert date in France, a Paris-based agency got a piece, and the same applied for all the other European countries. Artists actually paid more in commissions in Europe than in the States due to this awkward arrangement, which still exists today, but not in as many countries as before.

Touring with orchestras both domestically and abroad presented new fiscal complications. Some of the time, the agency representing the orchestra was not the same one that took care of me. And of course, each of those management companies was more than happy to have someone from its own roster as the soloist. This held true not only in Europe but also in Asia as well as the United States. To simplify, or complicate, depending on your point of view, I might be on tour with the St. Louis Symphony, but the tour would be arranged and managed by CAMI. Although I was an ICM artist, I was engaged for the tour by the orchestra, not the agency. I still had to pay commission to my management company, despite its lack of involvement, but at least I did not have to turn over a chunk of money to the company booking the orchestra.

Shelly Gold died unexpectedly only a few months after I had signed on with ICM, and after a very bitter struggle within the company, Lee Lamont emerged as chief executive. She was tough and could take on anyone. But under that armor was a very sweet person who cared deeply about her clients. She assigned me to Jenny Vogel, who would move out to Los Angeles, where ICM founded a West Coast division just to keep her in play. This all worked quite well. Lee made the big decisions, and Jenny put out feelers and followed up with phone calls.

By then I was music director of the National Symphony Orchestra (NSO) in DC. Things could not have been going better. In 2000, I became chief conductor of the BBC Symphony in London, splitting most of my time between the two cities. But the following year saw another set of changes, one, of course, that would affect the world on 9/11. Lee retired shortly thereafter and was replaced by David Foster, whom I only knew slightly. Jenny continued on, working to keep continuity in the company.

The lack of a true relationship with the new boss caused a very awkward situation that ultimately prompted me to make an important decision. The NSO and I were in New York, presenting Beethoven symphonies with Gustav Mahler's "retouchings" at Carnegie Hall. There was a lot of interest in this project, and the concerts were sold out. I even got my first byline in the *New York Times* for an article I wrote about the endeavor.

Walking along 56th Street, headed for the hall, I saw David coming from the opposite direction. We greeted each other, and then he uttered the words that would change my managerial life: "What are you doing in town?" I could have been nice but instead chose a very atypical answer, at least for me. "I have a concert with the NSO at Carnegie, and ICM is handling this event." He kept his cool, but right then and there I decided that if the head of the company did not know what his artists were doing, then I should not be with the agency anymore. With Lee Lamont out of the picture, there was little reason for me to stay other than Jenny, but when I told her of my decision, she understood.

The very next day, I called my longtime friend Doug Sheldon, the leading representative at CAMI. We had lunch, and I signed on with his company. Almost thirty-five years after being shown the door by Ronald Wilford, who was still active, I came to be with the agency that had turned me down. Doug would prove to be a smart manager. He had some of the biggest names in the business, ones that brought in significantly more cash to the company than I did.

Still, relationships with most orchestras were flourishing, and running my career was not so difficult. After a couple years, Doug proposed a unique idea. He wanted to represent me in all my conducting activities worldwide—no more Askonas Holt in London or KD Schmid in Hannover. Even Asia would be under the CAMI wing. The internet was developing, so why bother to go through several agencies when one person could do the job just as easily? My other representatives were not thrilled with this consolidation, but I thought it made sense at the time. I was wrong. Without actual boots on the ground, it was just too hard to make inroads or continue associations, because CAMI did not have solid relationships with all the orchestras around the globe.

I was shut off from the London scene, an area where I had been booked continually since 1974. Orchestras were searching for the next young conducting star, and those of us who had been in the trenches were either forgotten or thought of as relics. Fortunately, I was asked to become music director in Lyon, France, and Doug handled this very well—maybe too well. After five years, cutbacks in the budget from the city government made my salary untenable. Even after concessions, my staying on might have required eliminating positions in the orchestra to cut costs. I would not allow that to occur and left after my sixth season.

During my time in France, I decided to return to the older formula of one agent in the United States, one in Europe, and one in Asia. But now there were many new faces at the management companies as well as orchestras, several of whom did not know me or what I had done in the past. Selling me was more difficult. I had recently turned seventy years old and was trying to figure out what to do with the remainder of my conducting life. Being on the go constantly was draining, and I was pondering the idea of relinquishing the administrative aspects of being a music director to focus exclusively on music-making.

Ronald Wilford died in 2015, after being with CAMI for fifty years. This caused enormous turmoil at the agency, eliciting a power struggle to see who would become the leader and what direction the company would take. Ultimately Doug lost, and for various reasons, he walked into the office on a Friday, said he was resigning, and took his belongings. Now I was without an agent in the States. But it did not really seem to matter. If orchestras wanted me, all they had to do was write or call directly.

Still, I thought that a little help was needed and turned yet again to an old friend, this time Jeff Berger. He had worked at CAMI as well as BMG (Bertelsmann Music Group), where he was involved in some of my recording projects. His bailiwick for the past couple decades has been in the world of Broadway, but he seemed interested in representing me. Along with my assistant in Detroit, Leslie Karr, we now have a trio that operates quite differently than in the past. We decide on a case-by-case basis what we will do and who will take care of securing those dates. I no longer have an interest in building a career. It is time to just enjoy music-making and life.

This tale is told with the hope that younger musicians will understand that the world of managers and agents is changing. It is not difficult to imagine that in say, ten years' time, artist management companies might very well have disappeared. Perhaps it is still beneficial to have someone to jumpstart the musical vehicle, but once you are on the road, remember that we now have self-driving automobiles.

The question regarding the appropriate time to secure the services of an agency is up to the individual artist. Your age is irrelevant, and you should always keep your best interest in mind. This is not a decision you should make by yourself. Inquiries should be run past your teachers and others who serve as mentors. Leave family out of it, as they will likely express a prejudice that could send you into freefall, even if they are musicians themselves. Unless you are a prodigiously gifted artist and very young, my advice is to wait until you have more or less completed your studies at conservatory, university, or music school. Try to dip your feet into the professional world before setting out on the hunt for a representative.

In recent years, some musicians have chosen not to have an agent but rather a personal assistant, who is more like a PR person. Publicity, via any of the existing digital platforms, is the watchword of our times. There are so many promotional tools that young conductors have access to today that simply did not exist during my formative years.

If I had one overriding recommendation that sums up my feeling about not only agents but also most aspects of life, it is this: Find someone you trust to look out for your interests. Learn from the voices of experience. And remember that an agent's first priority is often to make money for the company.

A new and problematic development has reared its head and created an even more difficult situation for artists. With the pandemic prompting the shutdown of major agencies as well as smaller-scale management companies, several avenues of exploration have been closed. I deal with this topic in the "Road to Recovery" portion of the book, but suffice it to say that all of us need to be more creative in how we manage our own paths forward.

7

ON DIVERSITY

You don't make progress by standing on the sidelines, whimpering and complaining. You make progress by implementing ideas.

—Shirley Chisholm

Perhaps the finest three years of my life were spent attending Los Angeles High School. It was seven blocks away from my house, so I could walk there, or take my Corvair when I was sixteen. Searching for a parking place might put me three streets away from the building, but hey, I had my license and, by God, I was going to drive whenever I could.

The school was in a district that encompassed students from various racial, socioeconomic, and religious backgrounds. We were a lesson in how young people could get along. I am speaking about the time period from 1959 to 1962, pretty much before the world would change in terms of, well, everything. During my entire time at the home of the Romans, very little attention was drawn to the differences between cultures.

We studied, played, and learned together. Our social and cultural disparities made little difference to us; we could both celebrate and make fun of those qualities that made us individuals. Sometimes during lunch breaks, some of us would jam into one of the smallish practice rooms and engage in something called a "chop" session, in which no topic was off limits. We could insult each other, trying to outdo the person who said something that today could get you suspended or even expelled from school. That is just how it was. My, how times and propriety have changed.

If there is one topic that is on the lips of pretty much everyone in the orchestral world, it is the subject of diversity. What was once the exclusive province of white males has been altered dramatically in a surprisingly short period of time. For some, these changes cannot come fast enough, and with that, we have found ourselves in some almost unnavigable waters.

My high school music groups were filled with the same variety of individuals as the whole school. About a mile away, there was Fairfax High, located within a mostly Jewish neighborhood. And to the east, there was Fremont, a predominantly Black school. This was partitioned because of the way the school districts were set up, and if you went to public school, you went to the one closest to where you lived. I was fortunate to have attended the most diverse school of the three.

Travel about five miles to downtown LA, and you only saw white musicians on the stage if you went to Philharmonic Auditorium. But go to the sound stages, jazz clubs, and recording studios, and you could find a balance of musicians that looked surprisingly like good old LA High. I would soon learn that the real world was not like this at all. But I was not prepared for the degree of segregation, mostly but not all unintentional, that existed in the orchestral world.

My first taste of this came when I was asked to join the union when I arrived in St. Louis as the assistant conductor. Since I already belonged to Local 47 of the American Federation of Musicians (AFM) in Los Angeles, it was not necessary for me to be part of the one in my new home. When the first inquiry was made, I was told that the number of the union affiliate was 2-197. I did not understand why there was a hyphenated set of digits and wanted to know why.

"Because Local 2, the second oldest union in the country, was for white musicians, and Local 197 was the separate union for Black musicians."

Gulp!

I discovered that this was not uncommon in the United States, and it was not until 1953 that segregated locals began to merge, starting with the amalgamation of Locals 47 and 767 in Los Angeles. To this day, I do not understand why both numbers are still included in some cities. Why not just one, equal union for all?

When I was appointed assistant conductor in 1968, only two members of the St. Louis Symphony were Black. That number has not changed by much over the years, and the same is true in most major orchestras. As difficult as it was for women to be hired, the plight of racial minorities was even greater. Most of you may not remember the time when only men played in the orchestra, with the occasional exception of a harpist. But at least that barrier came crashing down rather quickly with the dawning of the screened audition.

The idea behind the use of the screen was that if no one could see the person auditioning for a position in the orchestra, then there could be no accusation of discrimination. This made perfect sense during the civil rights movement and continued into the equal-rights era. But today, questions about this practice are coming up, many that seemingly have no satisfactory answers.

Check out how your orchestra looks onstage at the present time. In many of our top-tier groups, you will see an almost equal number of women performing with their male colleagues. This certainly was not the case even ten years ago. Indubitably, the screen has made a difference in this area, considering that the United States has not exactly been the paragon of equality between men and women. After all, twelve states still have not ratified the ERA, and the #MeToo movement has exposed the persistence of sexual harassment in the workplace.

But times have changed. It is my belief that very few women would be discriminated against on the basis of their gender in the orchestral hiring process today, with judging based on how musicians play, not how they appear. In a way, the screen now represents a bit of an insult to those who are making the decision as to who will join the orchestra. Do we really believe that musicians of today cannot come to a fair conclusion irrespective of the candidate's gender and race?

Perhaps more to the point is that the screen takes away certain parts of the musical experience that musicians will encounter in the actual job. We do not rehearse or perform behind a barrier. Why should we have it there for auditions? Yes, anonymity would be compromised, but usually, one or more members of the orchestra know who is auditioning anyway. I certainly have had moments when I knew who might be playing, even though there was no paperwork confirming the identity of the person behind the wall.

Here is an example of how inequitable the screen can be: when there is a wind or percussion vacancy, or an opening for a titled chair, the people on the audition committee typically include those who are in the section in question. So if you have a vacancy for first flute, and the second flute of the orchestra tries out for the position, the committee automatically knows that this colleague is auditioning. How? Because that person is supposed to be in the hall listening and is not there, so logically the panel assumes that this musician is one of the candidates playing. Add to that the members of the orchestra who are usually advanced straight to the finals and chances are that most jury personnel can figure out when that particular musician is playing. As trained professionals who have rehearsed and performed together over a number of seasons, they know how their musical colleagues sound.

The same prejudicial matters can arise when a candidate is a student of one of the members of the orchestra. Certainly the teacher will have coached the younger musician through the rigors of the audition and how to best prepare and perform. And what of those players who have served as extras and substitute musicians throughout the years? Everyone knows how they play and act as citizens in the orchestral workforce. Then you have those string players who may have tried four or five times and failed to make the cut. Magically, one of them finally gets in, but it is all in relation to the others who played on that given day. It is not in the context of their previous efforts. A baseball player who hits .200 is not going to make the team. Add to all that the question of what other industry hires anyone without knowing about his or her background and the dilemma becomes even clearer. There is no true fair doctrine, at least in practical terms.

In addition, the anonymity of the candidates leaves us without critical information we should have when listening. Experience is often at a premium in the audition pool. Most musicians who have been in an orchestra for many years are not interested in moving to another city. They may not have taken an audition in a long time, and it is possible that they are not as technically capable as when they began their careers. But it is their service that brings an important element to an orchestra, and this needs to be taken into account. We do not need to know their names or ages, but an important aspect of the audition process is having a CV to at least see where these musicians have worked previously.

Of course, these are unusual examples to highlight, but they are indicative of the problems encountered in today's musical marketplace—which brings me back to the diversity issue. For the past several years, the League of American Orchestras has been focusing on how to bring more African Americans into the world of symphonic musicians. And many orchestras offer programs that give the equivalent of scholarships to people of color. In Detroit, for instance, one or two musicians can play in the orchestra for two years, but when the fellowship program ends, they get thrown right back into the pack of the jobless.

But suppose budding orchestra musicians from underrepresented communities are discouraged from pursuing the profession because they feel the stigma of discrimination. Often, when I speak to students of color, they tell me that they have been warned off by some about the prospect of entering the musical workforce with the odds stacked against them. There are no reparations in the music world. We can, however, alter the audition process, just a little, to help ensure the highest quality while encouraging everyone of ability.

Here follows the Slatkin Audition Process (SAP):

All applicants submit their CVs for consideration as has been the usual method.

A round of preliminary judging takes place, either in the form of in-person auditions behind a screen, or through recordings that are listened to by the audition committee. Again, this is the normal route today.

After that, the orchestra holds an in-person semifinal round, without the presence of the music director. The difference is that the screen is taken down, no matter the number of contestants. Among other factors not discussed above is the right of a candidate to see the space into which he or she will play. I actually find that this is one of the most compelling arguments against the screen. As a listener, I want the performer to feel at ease and know what the hall looks like and how it sounds without a barrier between that person and the jury.

Having explained why I do not care for blind auditions, I think it is important to point out that many musicians were appointed to orchestras via this route. They believe, in many cases, that they might not have been given the job if the screen was not in place. We cannot know if this is true, simply because there is no way to compare what it might have been like with the barrier out of the way.

My proposal is to keep the screen for the first round, but to remove the barrier and allow interaction in the semifinal round. The combination I am suggesting is a compromise that I believe is worth trying. With feedback allowed in that second round, the experience could actually be helpful to musicians who do not advance. They would potentially leave with information that could prove useful for the next audition.

Let's say that the audition committee boils it down to three or four musicians. Are you ready for the really big change? Here it is: there are no finals in the traditional sense! Instead, each of the candidates who passed through the semifinals is invited to play with the orchestra for four weeks. It does not matter what the position is—we will know in that time whether someone is good enough to become a member of the ensemble. String players can rotate among different chairs so that all the other members of the section have an opportunity to express an informed opinion.

After all the candidates have completed the trial period, the audition committee meets with the music director to present observations and opinions on their qualifications. The leader of the section in question and the conductor reach a final decision, as it used to be a long time ago. There is no vote, as any judgment in music is subjective and each person brings their own personal feelings into the mix.

What many people do not know is that once a musician gets into the orchestra, there is a probationary period, which can last up to a year and a half. During that time, the player can take a leave of absence if employed by another orchestra, thereby retaining a position in the former ensemble while awaiting a tenure offer. This is unfair to the originating orchestra, as it cannot hold auditions until a verdict is rendered by the potential new group.

Therefore, I am going to suggest that the tenure period be shortened to four months, during which time a group of musicians meets with the probationary player monthly to give input and feedback along the way. We do not need a year and a half for this, as it only delays the situation for the future, should a person decide not to accept the position after that time. We must think of what is good for the orchestra and not the player who might be coming from another group.

How does this process help in terms of diversity? It seems to me that a decision can be made in favor of a candidate who represents an underserved community if the jury members feel that the player's musicianship is on par with the others being considered. In this case, the diverse player has an edge, increasing the potential to inspire other minorities to the stage. The candidate of color contributes added value by bringing the orchestra a step closer to reflecting the diverse community it serves, which will ultimately lead to a stronger and more sustainable organization.

This is not a perfect solution, by any means, but it is a start in encouraging more people of color not to give up because of the process. In my heart, I truly believe that the days of overt discrimination in the music world are over, although unconscious biases are more difficult to recognize and resist. In my experience, when one member of a jury does not care for an applicant for personal reasons or expresses an inflexible viewpoint, this is almost always counterbalanced by other fair-minded musicians on the committee.

We can all agree that any musician hired for an orchestra job must meet the requirements of solid musicianship, first and foremost. This can only start with an early introduction and continued study of music, beginning at home and in the schools. Orchestras should do everything in their power to encourage programs that bring this learning to the fore in their communities. With less and less government support going toward arts initiatives, it is up to the professionals to step in and work hand-in-hand with schools to develop programs that expose children to the sounds of an orchestra and provide consistent, high-quality musical instruction.

Education is essential to increasing diversity in the classical music field, and that also applies to those who attend or listen to concerts. While young people naturally gravitate to styles that are listened to by their peers, music appreciation tends to be something that is passed down through the generations.

I believe that orchestras should make every effort to increase accessibility for as many people as possible. This comes about through judicious ticketing prices, creating a more user-friendly environment in the concert hall, and allowing for a shared experience among the audience. In my view it is not merely a question of programming but rather the manner in which the music is presented. For example, more and more musicians are becoming comfortable speaking to the audience. This is critical if we truly desire to engage new concertgoers and include more people in our art form. At the same time, we cannot pander to extraneous visuals to make our points. One of the things that makes the world of the concert hall so special is that it offers an abstract experience. Everyone can create their own images as they listen. It is our job to show them how.

There is a reason I have not discussed female conductors or composers so far. That is because they are already making significant progress in the field. Orchestras and opera companies are going out of their way to be more inclusive, sometimes to the point of overdoing it. There may come a day when the gentlemen start to complain about discrimination against their gender. Tough. It has been a long, hard road for the ladies. For the next few years, we will see and hear their voices. Time will judge how their artistry will be accepted.

Marin Alsop once said in an interview with the *New York Times* back in 2005: "I assumed there would be an influx of women on the podium, but there are not many more at my level than there were twenty years ago. Maybe boards don't want to hire women because they don't meet the archetypal image of the maestro."[1]

Today, it remains true that none of the so-called great orchestras has opted to engage a female music director. However, more women are applying and getting into conservatories and music schools than in my student days. This increase in representation in the training ground is an important component in fostering a diverse pool of applicants being considered for major posts.

Ultimately, opportunities given to music directors, and conductors in general, must be based on the quality of the results they achieve. Either one is a good musician or not. However, the "woke" culture applies to the musical world as well. Social demands have their place in the arts, as everything we do reflects how things were, are, and will be in the world at large.

Female composers have also made great strides in recent decades. For far too long, women were relegated to the realm of performer, and even then, history did not favor those artists. It was only in the later part of the 20th century that women were recognized for their achievements in composition. All of a sudden, we started hearing of voices from the past who had gone unrecognized or were acknowledged only as footnotes in history. In response to calls for an evaluation of the output of these composers, we started to see an emphasis on the much-needed diversity in programming.

Works by female composers are now performed by the major orchestras and opera companies, although still not in the numbers of their male counterparts. At this time, men outnumber women by almost ten to one in the field, even in conservatories and universities, but those numbers will hopefully change with a greater influx of music created by women.

As noted, female conductors have yet to make it into the upper echelon by becoming music directors of the top-tier orchestras. That will come soon enough. At least one opera company, San Francisco, has chosen a woman to lead the theater. Hopefully, she and eventually her compatriots will not be seen as women but simply, or complicatedly, as just conductors. I cannot wait for that day.

p.s.

A version of this chapter was made available to the public prior to the printing of this book and just after an article about the topic appeared in the *New York Times*. The lively debate that followed Anthony Tommasini's piece "To Make Orchestras More Diverse, End Blind Auditions"[2] and the publication of my essay on the cultural website Slipped Disc[3] was unlike any other I had seen in the classical music workplace. My thoughts are meant to begin a discussion that should have taken place long ago; there are many directions forward on this path, and I applaud those who are working tirelessly to prioritize equity and inclusion in the classical music landscape.

8

ON SOLOISTS

Technique is really personality. That is the reason why
the artist cannot teach it, why the pupil cannot learn it,
and why the aesthetic critic can understand it.

—Oscar Wilde

They are the stars who draw in the public. Their larger-than-life
personas might eclipse the talent they possess. What they wear
is sometimes as important as what they play. The soloist can be the
best friend offstage and the worst enemy on.

Such is the enigmatic role of the instrumental or vocal vir-
tuoso. Most of the time, soloists exhibit few of the negative traits
mentioned above, but when they do, there is palpable tension from
center stage to podium. Even the orchestra feels it, whether during
rehearsals or at the concert itself.

At one time, it was rare for a soloist to dominate the platform.
The conductor, or ensemble leader, was in charge of everything,
and if the program happened to include a concerto, this was simply
another part of the performance and not a highly publicized event.
Things began to change when opera started promoting a few singers
of note, particularly in the time of Mozart. Young Wolfgang Amadeus himself might easily be described as the first instrumental soloist
to call attention to himself when he performed on either violin or
piano.

From there, works for soloist and orchestra blossomed, placing composers like Beethoven, Brahms, Schumann (both Clara and

Robert), Liszt, and Paganini in the spotlight. In fact, Paganini's charisma was reportedly so strong that women swooned and fainted during his performances. He would have been quite at home in Las Vegas.

As the 19th century came to a close, an important change emerged—composers performed their own works less and less frequently. With the advent of recordings, instrumental soloists such as Josef Lhévinne, Vladimir de Pachmann, Josef Hofmann, and so many others would become household names. They could be heard on rolls, shellac, and eventually vinyl. The same was true for the singers. Enrico Caruso dominated the charts, and those who could not hear the tenor in person were content to hear him on their new playback devices.

Probably the last truly great artist to serve as soloist in his own compositions was Sergei Rachmaninov. My grand uncle, Modest Altschuler, played an important role in introducing American audiences to Rachmaninov's work, having conducted the Russian Symphony Society of New York in the US premiere of the Second Symphony in January 1909. During Rachmaninov's debut tour in America, Altschuler conducted his Second Piano Concerto at Carnegie Hall featuring the composer as soloist. Not only was Rachmaninov one of the world's most remarkable pianists but he also excelled as a conductor. Consequently he was offered the music directorship of the Boston Symphony Orchestra. Remember that it was only in the mid-19th century that conducting became a truly independent profession.

Over time, the great soloists and composers began aligning themselves with artists whose baton skills might make their works more common throughout the world. For instance, in the 1920s, Rachmaninov began a mutually influential association with Leopold Stokowski and the Philadelphia Orchestra. His relationship with that group continued through the Ormandy era, and he recorded all five of his works for piano and orchestra with those two conductors.

When such soloists as Jascha Heifetz, Arthur Rubinstein, Vladimir Horowitz, and Mischa Elman came to America, there were battles over who would conduct their debuts. Arturo Toscanini, in particular, became the go-to conductor, as he had a reputation for being the most influential at the time. Even his acolytes, such as

Bruno Walter, took second place when it came to introducing new repertoire and artists.

Increasingly, composers began writing great works intended for soloists other than themselves to perform. Perhaps it was because tastes had changed, and instead of folk music and religious hymns, we now had the world of popular song and jazz. Usually these works were created by the performing artists or came via Tin Pan Alley, the pipeline for short pieces in the vernacular. George Gershwin, Cole Porter, Scott Joplin, and so many others were the 20th-century equivalents of Verdi, Mozart, and those composers whose tunes might be sung or hummed by everyone in the street.

Once the conducting profession was fully established, stick handlers for the most part stayed away from presenting their own compositions in public, with the significant exception of Leonard Bernstein, who rose to prominence while actively pursuing a dual career in conducting and composition. In the 20th century, composers Igor Stravinsky, Aaron Copland, Paul Hindemith, and Benjamin Britten were practitioners of both creation and re-creation, and Pierre Boulez, John Adams, and Thomas Adès continued this trend. However, it was very rare for an instrumental soloist to also embark on a career at the podium.

Most of us who conduct have done some composing. I realized fairly early on that I had little to say in terms of creating original music, but at least I learned how to orchestrate. I started when I was just sixteen years old, studying with Mario Castelnuovo-Tedesco, teacher to the great composers of Hollywood. For three years, it was a fugue a week plus assorted exercises in voice leading and writing for various instruments. By the time I entered The Juilliard School in 1964, I had both legs up on almost every other classmate.

Having passed on my early goals of becoming a violinist, pianist, violist, and even composer, I settled into the conducting program. My teacher at Juilliard was Jean Morel, a very old-school musician who had few compliments to offer anyone, especially his students. His thought process was simple: if it was good, there was nothing to say, but if it was not, then a thorough wiping of the floor was in order. I was used to it from my own upbringing, but there were times when some of his students would leave the classroom in tears.

Despite his uncompromising teaching methods, Morel was a great collaborator with the soloists when he was conducting a concerto. His technique was beyond clear. It embraced an elegance coupled with precision that in my mind is still unmatched. Sharing a campus with Itzhak Perlman, Pinchas Zukerman, Emanuel Ax, and other future luminaries, we conducting students had ample opportunity to hone our collaborative skills.

I use that word "collaborative" rather than "accompanying." Although works in the concerto form always list the solo instrument first, it is important to remember that the additional "and orchestra" is still in the same font and style. Soloist and ensemble must exist as partners in order to produce a unified performance, regardless of repertoire.

I have often been asked who has the last word in a concerto. My answer is that the soloist has the authority. This artist may have a handful of concerti in his or her current repertoire, while the conductor has more than a hundred pieces to lead each season. The soloist might play the same concerto six or seven times in a year, in contrast to the conductor, who may only present that particular piece once. Clearly it is the person standing (or in the case of pianists, sitting) near the front of the stage who has the final say about how a piece will be performed. The conductor might suggest a few alterations to phrasing or balance, but in a concerto, the soloist rules.

Usually, the person front and center will meet with the conductor prior to the first rehearsal. I insist on two sessions with the soloist and orchestra to get familiar with the artist's approach to the work before running through it again at the dress rehearsal. When a member of the orchestra is the soloist, I try to give the musician three tries at it, as this is relatively uncharted territory, even for the concertmaster. Conductors should strive to support musicians in this position and make them as comfortable as possible.

Sometimes there is little or no rehearsal time for the concerto. Yes, I said no rehearsal. If a soloist falls ill and a musician steps in at the last minute, the best we can do is meet ahead of time and just go through the tricky spots. With artists that I work with on a regular basis, very little time is needed for such a meeting, even if we have not previously performed the piece. We have lived and breathed music for much of our lives, and the pleasure of making music usually produces a fine performance because we know each other so well.

Young soloists can be a different matter altogether. They have limited experience, so the conductor takes on the role of teacher as well. I have led some classes with piano and conducting students in which we discuss how to successfully collaborate. For example, there might be a passage, such as a chromatic scale in a Beethoven concerto, in which the conductor has trouble catching the final note. When that happens, I ask the pianist to play it alone and invite all those in attendance to clap once when they think the pianist arrives at the last note. Most of them, even those pianists who play the work, miss this as well. What it tells us is that as soloists, many budding musicians have not yet learned how to navigate the muddy waters and decipher how their part fits into the whole.

Surprisingly, if I ask the orchestra to try the same exercise—listen once and then catch the run without the conductor—they will more than likely hit it dead on. As an ensemble, they are used to being flexible and attuned to subtle variation, as this is what they must do as members of the orchestral ranks. There have been numerous occasions when the group has saved the conductor total embarrassment, and I am speaking of not only the young maestri but also some of the greatest names in the field.

Once in a while, a critic will point out that during the concerto portion of a concert, I rarely looked at the soloist. The journalist will construe this as a sign that I was not in contact with that person, and therefore the collaboration was unsuccessful. Morel taught us at a very early point in my studies that music is a profession for the ears, not the eyes. There are really only a few points in most concerti where seeing the soloist matters. If it is someone I know well, the glances are made to acknowledge something that we found interesting and different from the rehearsals. This is usually unnoticed by both audience and orchestra alike. It is a sign of a very good performance.

In essence, musical partnership is all about listening. Sometimes the soloist will even interact directly with the orchestra members, as if they were leading the performance. I have no problem with this, and in fact consider it an indication of how involved everyone is. Of course, it is another matter when the soloist is inexperienced or has quarrels with the conductor. Fortunately, I am at an age when I mostly get to work with musicians whom I know and love.

I can only recall a couple of occasions when I have disagreed with the *star de nuit* and had to resort to having the artist pulled from the program. More often, soloists have to cancel due to illness, injury, travel delays, or visa problems. Usually we find someone else to jump in at the last minute, and once in a while, we have to change the concerto, virtually sight-reading it at the performance. On one occasion, my dear friend John Browning and I were scheduled to perform Prokofiev's Third Concerto with the Philadelphia Orchestra at their summer home in Saratoga. There was just one rehearsal for this concert, and when we arrived at the venue, the music on the stands was that of the same composer's Second Concerto.

This is not a piece that one does without proper preparation on everyone's part. Indeed, there are almost as many notes for the soloist as there are words in *War and Peace*. What to do? We asked if they could send the parts for the Third Concerto from Philly. Since John and I performed the piece often, and it was a repertoire item for the orchestra, we would sight-read it at the concert. It was one of the best performances the two of us ever gave of this work.

If the disagreements with soloists are significant, whether due to technical insufficiencies, wrongheaded musical thought processes, or temperament issues that create tension onstage, then a discussion must take place to determine if the soloist or conductor should step away from the performance. My method is to try to be accommodating, but on the rare occasions when that has been impossible, I have approached the management and requested a change. It probably helped that I had an established career and therefore greater leverage. I hated doing this, but in these cases the soloists were so out of the ballpark that I could not have managed anything close to a decent job of collaboration.

For the most part, I have been finding that soloists today are sounding more and more alike, with the exception of those who take artistic liberties to an extreme. A few artists today are making careers out of being different, and in my opinion, not in a good way. They tend to exaggerate phrases, improvise passages against the intentions of the composer, and fabricate tempi and dynamics to their own tastes. Call me old-school, but there is something to be said for preserving tradition. Music evolves, but this process is slow and should still be rooted in history. When artists distort a work just because they feel like it, I think it does a disservice to the public and the composer. I don't mind a reworking of masterpieces for the sake of jazz or pop renditions. However, I object to instances when the soloist, and even the conductor, purposefully pull the music into directions never intended by its creator. This type of self-promotion is just not a good idea in the world of classical music.

David Prudent, a piano performance major at Southern Illinois University, Carbondale, made a very interesting set of observations in response to a query I posed about the ideal collaboration between conductor and soloist, and what should happen when they truly disagree:

> The two roles feature many various aspects that can influence the answers to your questions. Is the soloist trying to start a career while the conductor is already an established figure in the orchestral scene, or is the conductor a young assistant or apprentice trying to gain credit by performing with a world-renowned soloist? Perhaps both are aspiring performers being given the chance to do a concerto, or maybe the conductor and soloist are both very famous and have actually worked together many times over decades-long careers.
>
> Concerning each individual's musical background, has the soloist had experience as an orchestral (or choral) musician in his/her training that can help them to understand the larger ensemble context? And has the conductor studied the soloist's part intricately enough on top of those of the orchestra? Sometimes, conductors may take the stage with the instrument they played as students. Often, conductors are, in fact, veteran soloists from before their time at the podium, and can speak from both viewpoints about this matter. These types may even conduct the orchestra from the keyboard (or other solo instrument) for the pre-Romantic concerto literature, as was done by the performers from those times (who were usually the music's composers, also).

One last dynamic that would be important in addressing this soloist-conductor relationship: the positional status of the conductor. Is the conductor the orchestra's music director? Associate/Assistant/Resident Conductor? Principal Guest Conductor? Guest Conductor? True, the soloist's relationship with the ensemble is also important, especially if he or she has played with them before, is in some sort of artist-in-residence standing, or is even an actual member of the orchestra, as is sometimes the case. But it is the conductor, and the conductor's position (if any) with the orchestra that can contextualize his or her input on the artistic direction of the orchestra's performance with the soloist, and of the rest of the concert, for that matter.

At the core of all of these factors, which will most likely vary from case to case, I think the relationship between soloist and conductor should be one of mutual respect and appreciation, each one knowing that, without the other, it would be impossible to perform this repertoire they both love. When they have a serious disagreement, they should put their artistic differences aside and try to focus on what the composer has indicated in the music, taking into account the style of other music by this composer, and that of relevant performance practice, while also calling on the orchestra more for their collective and diverse opinions and expertise. As for the narrowing of musical approach you mentioned, I would suggest a helpful macro-level response might be to change the programming, instead of the playing, of the musical scene by mixing it up with more underrepresented music from the past, and premieres of contemporary music. Not only could this lessen the overdoing of the standard works, which has contributed largely to the lack of diversity in interpretations, but it would push musicians and audiences to better appreciate the more standard repertoire.[1]

From my perspective, skilled conductors must be able to work successfully with many soloists. Perhaps their technique may not be the best, but the sheer force of their personalities and chemistry with the orchestra can elicit a wonderful result. In some ways, I enjoy a fine collaboration with a soloist even more than a terrific performance of a large-scale symphonic work.

9

ON MUSIC DIRECTORS

> I don't feel that the conductor has real power. The orchestra has the power, and every member of it knows instantaneously if you're just beating time.
>
> —Itzhak Perlman

Three words that encapsulate how maestri of earlier generations got such incredible results are fear, temperament, and leadership. Each of the greats had key traits in common. Although their work ethic did allow for moments of levity and the very occasional burst of humor, these instances were few and far between, and there was nothing that the members of the orchestra could do about it.

The music director, as the role exists today, is almost an entirely different animal than it was in the first half of the 20th century. In those days, for the most part, music directors were at home with their orchestras for the majority of the season. Almost none of them retained a second position with another ensemble, and their guest conducting schedules were limited by the shorter performance seasons as well as the travel options at that time.

More importantly, conductors such as Arturo Toscanini, Eugene Ormandy, Wilhelm Furtwängler, Serge Koussevitzky, and so many others wanted to focus their attention on one ensemble, building and molding the profile and sound to their own satisfaction. These conductors were relatively free to hire and dismiss musicians, sometimes for the flimsiest of reasons. My father told me about the time when Fritz Reiner was the conductor at the Curtis

Institute of Music. While rehearsing a full string orchestra version of Beethoven's *Grosse Fuge,* he went through the double bass section, player by player, asking each musician to play a particular passage. No one met his approval and he dismissed them all, doing the performance without those instruments.

If a wayward moment of inattention were to occur, a conductor could just tell the offending musician that his services would no longer be required in the orchestra. Hiring was usually done by the music director in consultation—sometimes—with the head of a given section. There were no audition committees. The word of the boss was final.

This ultimate authority is not prevalent today. Understandably, orchestral musicians and their union have introduced rules, restrictions, and contractual language to protect against abusive behavior. But with these necessary modifications to what was the norm came unintended consequences, mostly related to questions regarding who could do what.

When I started my career in St. Louis back in the late 1960s, the music director was the sole arbiter of what the orchestra would look and sound like. Programs for the entire season were devised in consultation with the administration, but the orchestra itself had little or no input into an upcoming season. Artistic advisory committees existed, but they had no real decision-making authority. Sometimes they were asked if there were any pieces of music they would like to play, but that was about it.

Gradually the purview of the artistic advisory committee increased, and musicians had more influence over who was chosen to conduct as well as the programs themselves. And what they asked for was in some cases amusing, simply because of the naiveté of the committee members. On one occasion they submitted a list of guest conductors they would like to see on the podium, a group that included Herbert von Karajan and George Szell. Never mind that both were dead. Dreaming big is always a good thing, but it is not helpful to the cause when the ideas are impossible to implement.

When I left the St. Louis position after seventeen years at the helm, the orchestra had garnered a fine reputation. I was part of a team that included a couple of outstanding executive directors and artistic administrators. I could not have done the job without them. But I knew that it was time to go. There were rumblings that some board members either felt a change of leadership was needed or had issues with my programming choices. I would not learn of the latter until after my departure.

In Washington, programming became a hotbed of contention. From my vantage point, the role of the music director includes guiding repertoire choices that represent the tastes of the individual conductor while finding a balance that keeps the customers satisfied. The nation's capital seemed like the obvious place to pursue an American music agenda. My predecessors did a decent job in this area, but the orchestra really did not reflect the image of an organization devoted to promoting the national cause.

When I took the reins, I programmed music encompassing all genres. My first concert as music director was all-American, including music by Duke Ellington, Claude Baker, Howard Hanson, and others. Claude's piece was based on texts by JFK and was narrated on that occasion by Ted Kennedy. The program reflected my feelings about the place of the National Symphony in the country's musical hierarchy, and I would continue to go down that path for the majority of my tenure. I was consistent, and maybe even aggressive, in that pursuit, sometimes antagonizing board members who wanted more focus on the standard repertoire. I left a lot of that to the guest conductors.

We toured abroad, playing music from our country in Europe and Asia. It constantly surprises me that most orchestras from America don't do very much to promote the music of their homeland when overseas. Would we not expect a French orchestra to include something from France? The Berlin Philharmonic and Vienna Philharmonic are always playing their great composers, as are all the orchestras from Russia. Okay, there are some great orchestras in cities where the composers are not so popular, such as Amsterdam or Hong Kong, but they are the exceptions rather than the rule.

This is when the authority of the music director truly used to come into play. Ormandy and Bernstein always promoted the music of the States at home, on recordings, and during tours. The fact that the majority of American masterpieces written during the 20th century were premiered by European conductors speaks volumes. Were it not for Reiner, Koussevitzky, Stokowski, and others, we would not have such a wealth of American repertoire.

These music directors understood the power of the podium when it came to programming choices. Frankly, I see little of that in today's leaders. Once in a while, music directors will take up a piece and perform it with their home orchestras, only to abandon the work when leading other ensembles. My predilection was to do as my predecessors did. When I found a piece that I loved, I played it everywhere. It not only brought attention to the composer but also carried the name of one of the orchestras that I led as music director, as the first performances were almost always with my home band.

One always has to remember that administrative control of an orchestra rests with the board of directors. They contribute money that pays the bills, and they make most of the nonmusical decisions. The relationship between the podium and the board leadership is complex. It starts with a honeymoon period, but as time goes on, things can change. There is usually turnover at the top of the executive branch every three years or so. Internal changes with the staff occur frequently as well, and sometimes you get the feeling that you have to start all over again.

Walking the thin line between the artistic world and the one in which the corporate sector is at the helm is difficult. The music director has to tailor his or her own artistic agenda to align with the overall direction and vision of the institution as articulated by the board chair. The lay leader's governance style can range from a distanced approach characterized by disciplined financial oversight to a hands-on methodology aimed at building relationships among all constituents of the organization. The music director needs to adapt his or her management strategies to complement each leader who comes to the fore as head of the board.

One trend worth noting has to do with procedures sometimes employed for judging how well a music director is doing. In the past, if the conductor was growing the orchestra and people were turning out to listen, that was the beginning and end of any discussion concerning contract renewal. Today, however, more board leaders are applying performance-review techniques that have worked well in the corporate workplace. One might find the conductor filling out questionnaires that attempt to evaluate the effectiveness of the music director by his or her relationship to all the departments in the organization.

I am not convinced of the efficacy of this method, as it discourages face-to-face communication when problems arise in favor of anonymous evaluation weeks or months later. Also, applying objective statistics to appraise performance might work well in the business sector, where achievement is often measured in numbers. Although we in the arts might be able to assess how well things are progressing in terms of increased attendance, for example, the subjective aspect of music-making is almost impossible for someone without formal musical training to gauge.

After fifty years as a music director, I decided it was time to step away from this role and just focus on making music. I felt an immediate sense of liberation. No more worries about the next committee meeting, auditions, box office numbers, or the like. It was as if all that I had done had led to this new chapter in my musical life. Even musicians who have known me for a long time noticed a newfound sense of freedom and a more relaxed, but still efficient, manner of conducting and rehearsing.

A whole new crop of music directors is out there now. Some come with a little experience, and others are just beginning this adventure. Several of them have sought me out, asking for advice about running an orchestra. Each ensemble is different, but I can share some guidelines with aspiring music directors that apply in almost all circumstances, at least in the United States.

First and foremost, know that you will be greeted enthusiastically for a while. What used to be called the seven-year itch is more like three in the orchestral world. If you are doing well, then there will be no need for the group to look for someone on the outside with whom to begin a new relationship. But over that seemingly short period of time, you will need to have demonstrated your ability to lead in every area. Conducting is not enough.

Without question, the next generation of music directors must continue to place priority on musical excellence. However, at the same time, I believe they must show leadership in the areas of diversity and inclusion, fundraising, and community engagement in order to succeed. Some fine examples of this versatility are evident today, especially in the so-called second- and third-tier orchestras.

Secondly, tread carefully on the issue of labor negotiations. Historically, most music directors have not gotten involved. Why should they? They do not have any say in the outcome. They are not even consulted when it comes to artistic matters that might go into a contract. But in recent times, this attitude has changed a little. Conductors have put out statements supporting the orchestra's position, while at the same time expressing hope that all will work out quickly. After a couple days, the music director goes into hiding again.

This approach has one big plus going for it. The orchestra will adore the conductor. Even if that person is not the best leader, he or she showed support, and the group will always remember that. The board members might not care for the gesture, but as they well know, it really doesn't alter the end result. Only so much cash can be raised, and unless the music director is really willing to go out there and hustle the bucks, he or she is sort of irrelevant to the negotiation.

Thirdly, pick your battles carefully. If you have ten ideas that you believe are great, count yourself lucky if you get one of them through the administrative pipeline. Always keep in mind that even though you lead the orchestra, it is the board that pays your salary.

Lastly, if you are taking a job in the United States, be part of the community. The jet-set life is certainly alluring, but there is no place like home. Maintain an even temperament and try your best to be a strong leader without alienating others. Mostly, just be yourself. If you have to make too many changes to your persona because of the job, you are in the wrong place.

10

ON RETIREMENT

I don't mind getting older. I'm enjoying not having that raging ambition I've had all my life.

—Jeremy Irons

It is the start of the concert season. The musicians are excited to be back, rehearsing for what they hope will be a wonderful opening concert. The management and staff have spent the past few weeks gearing up for all the activity that is about to commence. The public is also looking forward to seeing and hearing the orchestra again, as if reuniting with their own family.

As with every other season opener, the audience may notice some differences from the last time the orchestra was onstage. A few of the musicians who performed just a few months ago are no longer present. They have been replaced by fresh faces, mostly younger. What happened? Did the missing players retire, or were they recruited by another orchestra? Did they depart voluntarily, or were they let go?

One of the questions I am often asked is, "How does a musician know when it is time to leave the orchestra?" After all the hard work they put into auditioning for a position and maintaining the highest standards, tenured musicians can take comfort in knowing that being dismissed from an ensemble is quite rare. It can require up to two years for a music director or administration to build up a sufficient case against an instrumentalist for such things as incompetence, inebriation (difficult to prove), or insubordination. In almost every instance, the judgment is made by members of the orchestra with the guidance of an arbitrator. Many of those sitting on a dismissal panel are certainly thinking, "Am I next?" Notably, in the United States, the age of an orchestral musician has no place in this process.

My mother set a fine example of discipline when it came to making a decision about retirement. I was just starting my career, and she was in her early sixties, when out of the blue she called to tell me she was putting the cello down and retiring from being a performing musician. She had committed to two weeks of film-scoring sessions with John Williams, and once she had fulfilled that obligation, the instrument would have a permanent home in its case, only to emerge when she was teaching.

My reaction was one of shock. "Mom, you still play fantastically. Why stop now?"

Her reply was classic: "I don't ever want people to say, 'I knew Eleanor Slatkin when she played well.'" That kind of self-control is rare.

She would go on to teach the students of János Starker at Indiana University while he was on tour. After that, she taught in Chicago before returning to Los Angeles, where she continued to guide musicians who came to play for her, whether pianists, wind players, or singers. They valued her musical opinion and knew that she would be tough but fair.

In Europe, the vast majority of performers in orchestras or opera-house pits are employees of the government, and each country establishes a retirement age—for everyone. Literally all working members of society must retire when they reach a certain age, usually in their mid-sixties. The problem is that there are some, if not many, musicians who are as capable in their sixties as they were when they entered the orchestra. This certainly is true for string players, some of the woodwinds, and a few percussionists. Some of the brass section members start to lose their chops when they are a bit younger.

You might wonder how I was able to work as music director in Lyon starting at age sixty-five. After all, I was a government employee, and even the staff and administration of the Auditorium had to adhere to the peer-group legislation. Somehow, when it came to the artistic head of the orchestra, the government turned a blind eye, opting for experience in my case.

On several occasions, musicians of the Orchestre National de Lyon would come to my office and tell me they would be playing their final performance with the orchestra that evening. It was usually said in a matter-of-fact way, and at first, I didn't know how to respond. Could it have been a health issue, something related to the family, or perhaps even dissatisfaction with the job? No; it was always just the way the system worked. At the concert's end, I would bring out a bouquet of flowers for the retiree, and there would be a party in one of the other large spaces in the building. That was it—we only saw them again when another member of the orchestra retired, but of course, many continued to teach privately.

In contrast to European countries, the United States has outlawed mandatory retirement policies for most professions. Writer Kerry Hannon explained American retirement guidelines succinctly in an article published by *Forbes*:

> In the early 1970s, about half of all Americans were covered by mandatory-retirement provisions requiring they leave their jobs no later than a certain age, usually 65. In 1986, Congress abolished mandatory retirement by amending the Age Discrimination in Employment Act.
>
> A few fields, however, are exceptions. Certain occupations that are either too perilous—such as military service or federal law enforcement agencies—and others that demand high levels of physical and mental skill (like air traffic controllers and commercial pilots) generally still have mandatory retirement policies.[1]

The notion that the job must "demand high levels of physical and mental skill" to justify a mandatory retirement requirement is open to interpretation, but the positions that qualify for exceptions usually involve safety concerns.

Athletes certainly know when their bodies give out and they can no longer participate in a productive manner. Then again, baseball players, for example, make several million dollars a year, so retiring at age thirty-five does not seem like such a bad deal. They usually wind up as television commentators, as product spokespersons, or working in some other aspect of their chosen sport.

An orchestral musician approaching retirement must confront a very personal decision involving financial readiness and the emotional implications of leaving a job that is intrinsically entwined with his or her identity. Also, there are repercussions for the ensemble. A retirement can affect the artistic quality of the whole group and deprive the orchestra of musicians with valuable advice to pass on to the younger players.

Is there a solution for the retirement dilemma, one that might be applied to all musicians around the world? I believe there is, but it requires a lot of fortitude to implement. Currently, when a contestant auditions for a position with an American orchestra, the decision to hire rests with a committee, one that usually, but not always, includes the music director. Once that musician has achieved tenure after a probationary period of one to two years, the role of the committee in the evaluation of the hired musician disappears. Orchestra members have virtually no accountability to the colleagues they play with day in and day out. That is what needs to change.

My suggestion is that the musicians themselves should decide if a fellow member of the orchestra is no longer able to perform at a level commensurate with the standards of the ensemble. In conjunction with the music director, the players could meet once every year and decide whether the musicians who have reached the point of collecting defined benefits should remain in the orchestra. This is asking a lot. Pinning judgment on someone you have worked with for so many years is overwhelmingly difficult. However, there would come a time when each member of the committee would be judged similarly.

Former Minnesota Orchestra cellist Janet Horvath cites an interesting method utilized in Canada that allows musicians to approach retirement at their own pace:

> The TSO (Toronto Symphony Orchestra) contract allows for different ways to retire. They allow the musician to be "grandfathered" out. That is, the musician gives notice of their intention

to retire, and they are allowed to play two half seasons. This gives the musician a chance to "get used to" the idea and to pursue and build other things or hobbies. I know of so many colleagues who died very soon after retirement. Going from the rigorous, set-in-stone schedule to nothing is extremely difficult for previous generations of musicians. For many of us it's our life, our identity, and getting used to a NON-micro-scheduled existence is very difficult.[2]

This seems like a well-reasoned way to make the transition to retirement more manageable. It is also possible to structure the reduced workload for those approaching retirement based on the various rotational weeks off for members of the orchestra. Engaging the seasoned veterans when other musicians have time off makes a lot of sense. It is certainly better than bringing in an endless parade of substitutes.

In other comments musicians have shared with me on the subjects of age and retirement, some have expressed frustration with the lack of interaction between mature players and younger members of the orchestra. Experienced musicians offer wisdom and high-level musical instincts that complement the technical prowess of their youthful counterparts. The advice and insight of an experienced stand partner can also help put the younger colleague at ease.

Maneuvering one's way through the myriad hurdles of the symphonic world is never easy. Perhaps administrators could be encouraged to engage a senior member of the orchestra to act as a mentor to the newcomers.

These days, orchestral musicians have more say in the everyday workings of the organization. Some sit on the board of directors as well as numerous committees that advise on everything from programming to travel. Why not ask the musicians to monitor the artistic welfare of the whole? Looking out for the interests of the collective while also making sure that no one is performing at a level below the skill set of the orchestra is a positive step.

In my final year at Juilliard, five of us who were about to launch careers in the profession came to an agreement. If the other four felt that the fifth person was no longer capable of the highest possible performance standard, we would tell that musician that it was time to rethink the future, no matter at what age. So far, two of them have changed course. They are still in music but not doing things that are beyond their current capabilities.

As for me, I will follow my mother's example.

III

THIRD MOVEMENT

11

ON REPERTOIRE

I have selective hearing.

—Eddie Van Halen

The life of a musician consists of a series of choices made throughout a lifetime devoted to bringing satisfaction to oneself as well as others. We are defined not only by how we do our job but also by the personal set of musical values that we develop and refine over the years.

Some of us devour as much music as possible, beginning from our childhood. As a kid in Hollywood, my exposure to different styles and genres contributed significantly to my persona throughout my conducting career. There were no boundaries. I was equally at home visiting sound stages, attending symphonic and chamber music concerts, sneaking into jazz clubs when I was underage, or poorly attempting to dance to the latest craze in rock and roll with my school pals.

My instrumental studies included violin, piano, viola, a bit of percussion, and even double bass. When everyone else wanted to be a drummer, I opted for producing actual pitches. In band I played the mallet instruments, allowing me to have the tunes all the time. In high school, we often played a piece by one Don Gillis, a composer favored by Toscanini. This delightful work was called "The January, February March." To this day, even though I have not heard it since the twelfth grade, I can still remember the melody clearly.

Some of my friends and I formed a sort of fusion rock and jazz group known as The Dead or Alive Five. We played at dances and tried out our improvisational chops. Once in a while, I might inject a bit of whatever piano piece I was working on at the time into the mix. In the orchestra, I was the first, and only, violist. Recently, when going through my LP collection, I came across a couple discs that were recorded from the annual winter and spring concerts. In the first movement of the Schubert "Unfinished" Symphony, just before the start of the cello tune that begins the second subject, one can barely make out a solitary Leonard, attempting the double stops that set up the rhythm under the elegant melody. My contribution is pathetic.

During these formative years, I also arranged songs for the annual musicals that were presented in the dilapidated auditorium of Los Angeles High School. Sometimes they would be for piano and string quintet, and on one occasion, I was allowed to augment with some winds and a drum set. This was also where I first got to conduct, and the orchestra director would sometimes let me take over part of a rehearsal for an upcoming concert.

What does this have to do with repertoire? Everything!

In my early experiences, I took every opportunity to learn what could and could not be done. I always tried to seize the moment and launch into whatever appeared on the horizon. After my father died and I resumed my musical expedition, most of my time was spent in the libraries of the university and then the music school I attended. But in those days, there was nothing to be found other than scholarly tomes, scores, and other writings devoted to what was simply called "classical music." The shelves contained very little about Ellington, Joplin, or even Gershwin. And this was in New York!

One had to travel to other places to get a fuller picture of the musical scene. In the Sixties we had the world of clubs, and I could occasionally sneak into places like Electric Circus to absorb current trends as they were sprouting. But it was the jazz scene that truly captivated me. I would go to Birdland, the Village Gate, and the Village Vanguard with a couple others from Juilliard who were hip enough to want to accompany me. We spent many an early morning listening to stories told by the jazz legends who appeared at these venues. Every one of these adventures would serve me well when I began as the assistant conductor in St. Louis. The hours of study in the libraries, excursions into New York's night life, and immersion in the film culture would begin to pay off.

Our country still did not have anyone other than Bernstein to represent a true American presence in the conducting world. But at least my generation had him to model ourselves after. Here was someone well versed in a variety of musical idioms. Plus, he had remarkable communication skills, something pretty much unheard of with the other maestri of the time. Bernstein's versatility cleared a pathway for a generation of homegrown talents who could exhibit multiple musical personas. No longer were we thought of as less worthy than our European counterparts. We were just different and more diverse in our choice of music.

Students starting out on the professional track undertake any opportunity that comes their way. It might be a Broadway show, a piece written by a friend at school, a small ensemble formed to help out a budding soloist, or all of the above. Nothing should be off limits as they start to find their way through the repertoire, old and new. In going through my own personal archive, I am astonished at some of the music I led in the earliest phases of my conducting life.

Assistant conductors, whether in the concert hall or the opera house, are expected to thoroughly know the music being performed. Perhaps anticipation of the day when someone falls ill and they are asked to jump in forces the issue—if they are not ready, then that opportunity may never come again. Retaining as much material in the mind as possible also becomes imperative. Every experience has some value later on. The power of recall comes in handy for conductors, even when they are older and more experienced.

In the summer of 2019, I was conducting in Aspen, a return to my student haunt, when I received a call from the artistic administrator of the New York Philharmonic. She informed me that Bramwell Tovey, who was scheduled to lead the orchestra in Vail, Colorado, had fallen ill. Could I take over? There were two programs to fill, one quite traditional and the other of music by Cole Porter. Originally the conductor was also going to play the piano for two of the songs, accompanying a soprano. It had been some time since I had done anything by the *Anything Goes* composer, but this music was in my bones.

The morning after my concert in Aspen, I was on the road to Vail. Arriving just a couple hours before I was due onstage, I sat down at the piano and practiced a little. Although my keyboard days are mostly behind me, everything went well at the single rehearsal with the orchestra and soloists. I hosted, conducted, and played the Porter show that night. The next day's program of Glinka, Rachmaninov, and Tchaikovsky represented quite a shift, to say the least. Many people were impressed that I could do this on short notice and with a certain degree of ease. This is just a recent example of the variety of musical experiences in my youth proving valuable, even more than fifty-five years after my student days in New York.

Given my somewhat eclectic musical tastes, it is surprising to me how many people attempt to pigeonhole my repertoire. Understandably, I am seen as a strong advocate of American music. Almost every orchestra I visit asks for something along these lines, and I am mostly happy to oblige. When I began my St. Louis tenure, I knew that pursuing this path could possibly lead to a limited set of choices when it came to dates outside of the Arch. When you are a music director, clearly you have to provide your orchestra and community with a broad canvas of pieces from all periods and styles.

Even with touring and recording, I kept pushing for the American composer, past and present. However, I also would bring the orchestra to New York with challenging works by composers including Peter Maxwell Davies, Nicholas Maw, Alberto Ginastera, and Luciano Berio, among others. We still managed to get a few staples of the canon onto the Carnegie stage, such as *Le Sacre du printemps,* Mahler's Third, and Bruckner's Second. The first program we performed in the hallowed hall contained music by Glinka and Ravel, plus the first New York performance of Shostakovich's cantata *The Execution of Stepan Razin.*

During my seventeen years at the helm, the good ship St. Louis made recordings for at least five different labels. With the exception of our Telarc albums, we continued to press on with American works. The very first recordings actually took place while I was still the assistant conductor and consisted of the complete works with orchestra by Gershwin. Stand-alone discs were produced by Nonesuch and New World Records, almost all of them featuring works by living composers. Then EMI came on board. There were no conductors on their roster from the States, and so we began to include some classics from America. Leonard Bernstein, William Schuman, Samuel Barber, and George Gershwin—again—made their way into the stores.

The last label we worked with was RCA, which was later bought out by BMG. This was the most productive relationship imaginable. We made more than thirty recordings together, and in 2018, with Sony now in the picture, a box set called *Leonard Slatkin: The American Collection* was released. It contained eleven discs with the Missourians plus two from Washington, DC. Surprisingly, the set did not include the two Barber recordings we created.

Meanwhile, on account of my family roots in Ukraine and Belarus, a great deal of my repertoire also featured works by Russian composers. I performed lots of Tchaikovsky and Rachmaninov all around the world. I suppose it is possible to make a career conducting the works of American and Russian composers exclusively, but European audiences were less interested in this programming. Many of my concerts in that part of the globe, even today, feature works from the Austro-Germanic world.

It was different in England. Aside from André Previn, there had not been a foreigner performing the English orchestral repertoire on a regular basis. This music had been a passion of mine for a long time, and I had the opportunity to perform and record it with the London Philharmonic, Philharmonia Orchestra, London Symphony Orchestra, Royal Philharmonic, and BBC Symphony. There seemed to be an eagerness on the part of British audiences to listen to their music as interpreted from a different, more global perspective.

Since I had studied with a French conducting teacher, Jean Morel, it made perfect sense for me to take the music director position in Lyon. I knew all the standard works from that country as well as some of the lesser-performed works by contemporaries of Debussy and Ravel. This background served me well, and I could throw myself into the music with abandon, just because I loved and cherished it.

Even though the recording market was eroding by the early 2000s, the upstart label Naxos managed to hang on. At that point, the prospect of classical musicians making money and advancing their reputations through recordings was severely limited. Nevertheless, I was already established as a recording artist, and Naxos gave me ample leeway to decide what I wanted to record. Perhaps that is why the label now boasts a complete collection of music by Leroy Anderson as well as William Bolcom's *Songs of Innocence and of Experience*. The Naxos catalog also includes a set of the complete orchestral works by Maurice Ravel performed by the Orchestre National de Lyon, which plays in an auditorium that bears the composer's name.

With recordings of Joseph Schwantner, Joan Tower, Donald Erb, Cindy McTee, Alla Borzova, Claude Baker, William Schuman, and so many others, I wound up covering a lot of territory, thereby putting my money where my mouth was. It's one thing to talk about devotion to a cause but quite another to be able to back it up with tangible product.

While I have made the case that the young conductor needs to know as much as possible in terms of repertoire, I believe it is important not to rush things. Getting through a Mahler cycle rarely means much until a conductor has fully absorbed and performed the music that came before it. It takes time to explore the depths reached by the greatest composers, which is why I believe it is crucial for burgeoning conductors to have pieces under their belts that are off the radar. By focusing on lesser-played music, they have an opportunity to take the time they need to digest works from the standard canon before presenting them to the orchestra and public.

This brings me to the final point. If I was starting out in the profession now, I would do exactly what I did fifty-five years ago: stake out repertoire that few are performing, keep presenting it to the public, and find that niche to make me different from others. But one has to truly believe in the composers and the music. Just doing it for the sake of being unique is hardly enough.

Find what you love and keep that flame burning.

12

ON MEDIA

There is no communication that is so simple that it cannot be misunderstood.

—Luigina Sgarro

"Mr. Watson, come here. I want to see you."
Our method of interacting with each other was changed forever when Alexander Graham Bell spoke those words in 1876 during the first phone call to his assistant in the next room. Could Bell, or Thomas Alva Edison, ever have envisaged what has occurred over the past century and a half? Edison could. After all, he had invented the first sound reproduction device in 1877 while working on improvements to Bell's telephone and Samuel Morse's telegraph.

The evolution of recording began with cylinders, followed by gramophone discs, 78s, 45s, 33s, and even 16s. Next up came the 8-track, cassette, and CD. Silent films gave way to sound, VHS, Betamax, LaserDisc, and DVD. The way we disseminated news and culture to the public exploded in the 20th century. The information age was pushing ahead at unlimited speed.

In music, it all started in 1888 with a recording of Sir Arthur Sullivan's *The Lost Chord*. The next year Johannes Brahms committed one of his Hungarian dances to cylinder. In 1890, Tchaikovsky's speaking voice could be heard. Peter Schram was the first opera singer to record, singing Leporello's aria by Mozart in Danish. Enrico Caruso had his first release in 1904.

Orchestras jumped into the growing commercial market during the first twenty years of the 20th century. Both in Europe and the United States, it seemed as if releases could not come fast enough. Conductors such as Leopold Stokowski, Arthur Nikisch, and Felix Weingartner took advantage of the new technology to advance their orchestras' profiles and expand touring options.

Arguably the biggest podium name, Arturo Toscanini began his long recording career in 1920. His early entries into the field provoked more and more product from almost every recording company out there. Record labels came and went. But RCA, Columbia, and others endured and started to reap large profits when they combined the income from popular music releases with their classical collections.

By the time I started recording, my parents had been at it for more than forty years. I was an eyewitness to the march of progress, seeing new techniques evolve almost daily. Whether it was on a sound stage, in a recording studio, or at home, the communication industry was in evidence all around me. Even at Juilliard, all performances were taped, and we students, unlike those from previous generations, could hear the result of our efforts.

The very first commercial recording I made was in LA on the 20th Century Fox lot. This was the same place where my dad had been concertmaster. Standing on the podium that day was one of the most moving moments in my life. And what did I record? The title music for a film called *Red Sky at Morning*. The music was by Billy Goldenberg, whose father was the percussion teacher at Juilliard.

The next recording I made was equally unusual. In December of 1973, a little film from Warner Brothers called *The Exorcist* came out. Unexpectedly, audiences lined up to get in, and all of a sudden, a soundtrack album was required. At the time, studios were saving money by utilizing music that already existed, as evidenced by *2001: A Space Odyssey*. In addition to the famous "Tubular Bells" by Mike Oldfield, the film also featured music by George Crumb, Anton Webern, and Krzysztof Penderecki. Warner's had its own record label, but they could not use existing recordings of works by the composers above because they had been issued by other companies.

The film opened on a Friday, and the next day, I got a call asking if I could fly to London and conduct the music at Abbey Road, with sessions starting on Monday. Warner Brothers paid for the round trip via Concorde, just to make sure I got there on time. After the first session, I was invited to dinner and a visit to a casino, where I played blackjack with Ringo Starr. It took three days to complete everything, even though there was not that much music. One would have thought that this would be a bestseller, but an argument between the director and the writer of the script over what the cover art should look like held things up. It was not until nine months after the movie came out that the soundtrack was released to an indifferent public.

In my fourth year as assistant conductor in St. Louis, music director Walter Susskind generously let me make the first discs to be issued during his tenure: the first integral cycle of the complete works of Gershwin for Vox Records. A new technique had come out at this time called quadrophonic sound. The system used four channels instead of stereo's two, requiring the listener to purchase another pair of speakers and get some other new equipment. For the *Cuban Overture*, we placed the Latin percussion instruments out in the audience in order to maximize the listening experience. This experiment did not last long. It turns out that we do not have four ears.

When CDs came into existence around 1982, we started to put seventy minutes of music on a disc as opposed to fifty for an LP. The new format provided more music for the customer's dollar, but this presented a real problem for orchestras. In the United States, we have recording sessions that last three hours each. A twenty-minute break is built into each hour, so in reality, it is just two hours of recording time. Although albums became longer, recording budgets did not increase. In effect, we had to tape more music in less time. It was exhausting and frustrating. And one more event would help seal the fate for recording orchestras in America: the collapse of Communism.

One person's crisis is another person's opportunity. Record companies were looking for less expensive ways to produce a musical product amid escalating costs. After the dismantling of the Berlin

Wall in 1989 and the fall of the Soviet Union in 1991, orchestras in the former Eastern Bloc were poised to enter the Western market.

For years I had a sweetheart deal with RCA. During the St. Louis years, I would make several discs per season, as well as others in London and Germany. In 1985, Red Seal was bought out by the Bertelsmann Music Group (BMG). It took a few years for the transition to stabilize, and by that time, Mr. Slatkin was going to Washington.

With my three-year contract at the National Symphony Orchestra (NSO), my manager was able to negotiate a ten-disc deal with the recording company. Unfortunately, after we made the first one, BMG pulled the plug, not only on me, but also on most of their other artists. Two more discs were released, but that was the end of it. For a while, I was convinced that my recording career was over. The same cutbacks in the States were being imposed by the other big labels as well.

Enter Klaus Heymann. In 1987, the Hong Kong–based German entrepreneur started a new label, Naxos. Clearly Klaus saw what was going on in the industry and found a unique way of cashing in. The company recorded prodigiously in places where the costs were minimal, and a flood of discs started showing up in the stores at half the price of those on the big labels. Klaus not only utilized orchestras in the former Soviet bloc, he also expanded the global recording industry to New Zealand and Australia.

The conductors and soloists were, for the most part, unknown. For the public, it seemed as though the name recognition of the artists was not nearly as important as what they were playing and how little the recording cost. In the meantime, almost all the American orchestras were shut out. Eventually, Klaus would negotiate deals with symphony orchestras in Seattle, Baltimore, Buffalo, and yes, Detroit. Usually these were tied to the collective bargaining agreement, so the fees paid to the orchestra were minimal. Naxos controlled virtually all the rights, with little or no royalties going to the ensembles. And trust me on this, the featured artists did not get much either. We were just happy to still be making recordings.

In order to make up for the lack of national or international exposure, some groups started forming their own recording companies. The London Symphony was the first to get this up and running, but soon a few enterprising American orchestras followed suit. Sales were not the driving factor, as it was more about keeping a physical product in the hands of donors, sponsors, and interested parties.

Enter the internet. At first, no one had any idea how symphony orchestras could utilize this outlet. Some footage of performances started appearing on YouTube without the authorization of the artists. To this day, I still can find some of my concerts on that platform that I never approved. It doesn't matter to me. With the industry in trouble, any kind of public forum is helpful.

In the second decade of the 21st century, the world of downloading and streaming came to the fore, and almost all the financial rules went out the window. I knew something was up when I went to buy a new car and discovered that a CD player was no longer offered, even as an accessory. It seemed as if anyone could get recordings out to the public with very little effort. Damn the lack of quality. But it is that control that is vital to keeping the soloistic and orchestral world alive. Detroit became the first symphony orchestra to make its concerts available for free online. This boosted ticket sales at home and gave the group a needed lift as it came out of the turmoil of a six-month strike.

Others tried to follow, but they could not do it. The American Federation of Musicians (AFM) had stringent guidelines and was not willing to bend them. At the very least, the union should have been understanding and encouraging of orchestras seeking to develop new formulas as recording opportunities disappeared. My thoughts are simple: The audience is whoever is watching or listening at a given time. Therefore, it is not limited to the people in the hall. And if the performance is broadcast or streamed for free, what difference does it make if the artists are not paid extra to reach more people? They still will perform at the same level in any event. While it is one thing to offer these livestreamed events without extra compensation for the artists, any rebroadcasts might come with a small surcharge attached. It is not detrimental to an organization to have more people watching and listening.

For a time, it looked like all was calm. Orchestra contracts were being settled well before their original expiration dates. Relationships between musicians and managements were, for the most part, amicable. Then March 2020 jumped all over us. It seemed that

Corona, another name for a fermata, put a real hold on everything imaginable. One by one, orchestras started canceling, at first weeks, then months, and eventually seasons at a time.

There were enterprising people, using very clever technological means, getting music out there. But it was not the same. Perhaps we might never return to what was known as normal, or maybe we might establish new paradigms of reaching the public and presenting our artistry. But some of the old bickering has started up again. How much should musicians and staff be paid if this was, indeed, an act of God? What would happen to those orchestras whose contracts would expire at the start of the next season? Will we ever bring the audience back?

Everyone is scrambling to figure out what comes next. The means by which we will start up again are unclear. Programming, which is usually set out a year and a half in advance, now sits in limbo. Whatever recording projects had been scheduled will have to be rethought, as the financial destruction to arts institutions will be immense. Perhaps some of you remember the film *Escape from New York* and its sequel, *Escape from L.A.* At the end of each movie, there are apocalyptic moments that cause humanity to start over. Snake Plissken is alive and well in the form of a virus.

For the world of the arts, we have at least established a foothold on the future. Technology will keep moving forward, and our ability to communicate will not disappear. Whoever figures out the next means of reaching the public by creating new paths of discovery will be forever remembered, just as Edison was.

13

ON COMPOSERS

Sometimes you just square the ball, and somebody else shoots, but some assists are so nice, and the passing is very important. We creators have a thing with the attackers.

—Kevin De Bruyne

Poor Bach—twenty children and still having to churn out a cantata every week. And what about his two wives? In Leipzig, where he held a prominent position as an organist, all those kids lived in a separate facility. He may have been able to remember the chord progressions in a complex keyboard work, but I wonder if he could recall all his offspring's names?

Haydn, Mozart, and Schubert each sat at a small desk with candlelight to compose symphonies, operas, chamber music, and songs. "Papa" managed to cram 107 of the first variety, 26 of the second, and 68 string quartets, as well as other works. All told, his output totals around 340 hours of music. Wolfgang, with 41 symphonies, 27 operas, and 22 string quartets, comes in at 220 hours. And Franz? With more than 600 songs, along with his other works, he had a total output of at least 1,500 pieces.

Beethoven seems like a piker—just 175 hours of music. What makes these statistics striking is the age at which the composers passed away. Haydn was 77, Mozart 35, Schubert 31, and Beethoven 56. Schubert probably wrote more notes than Mozart and in a shorter lifespan.

Whatever your age now, imagine putting all those tones to page, notwithstanding possible writer's block and hand cramps. In addition, with the exception of Haydn, writing music was not their only job. They were instrumentalists and even took on odd jobs to supplement the mostly meager earnings from their compositions. Haydn, however, was an exception because he was appointed composer to the various courts of the time, which provided him with lucrative, full-time work.

Today's composers for the concert hall write perhaps three pieces per year, if we are being generous, a productivity rate that pales in comparison to the aforementioned masters. The fact that the creative process has been made more efficient by computer programs that allow for the quicker entry of notes seems not to have made that much difference regarding output. Still, it never ceases to amaze me that a composer seemingly grabs a creative idea out of nowhere, translates it into a physical product, and produces something magical.

The job of those of us who are performers is to produce interpretations that breathe life into the music. After all, what is music on a page? Nothing but a set of circles and lines with the occasional instruction about volume, expression, and tempo. The remainder is up to us to figure out. That is one of the joys of being a re-creator. In some ways, the study process is a bit like working on a puzzle. We have these differing elements in front of us and somehow must sort them out to make a coherent picture in sound.

When I was a young person, well before considering any type of career, my parents hosted composers galore at my family's home. Because of their professional work, Mom and Dad were very busy playing music by people writing for film, string quartet, and popular recordings. Los Angeles served as a creative melting pot for the music business, and my folks were among the go-to people when it came to presenting the latest efforts in the various fields. In those early days, I never really thought about the creative process. As I played and read music, I accepted it as a finished product, without much consideration as to how it came to be.

Once I began my own composition studies, it became clear that writing music required rigorous study and practice. Doing exercises correctly was almost like mathematics, at which I continue to be dreadful. It wasn't until I was sixteen that I began to develop creative skills in music. Writing prose was something I had done since grammar school, but learning about voice leading, figured bass, and rhythmic complexities had not been on my radar. Between actual studies of these and a surprising knack for being able to improvise on the keyboard, my re-creative world in music started to take on a different dimension.

After high school, I spent a very short period of time at Indiana University as a composition major. However, the classroom environment was not my cup of tea; I was used to working with teachers on a one-to-one basis.

During the Vietnam years, the threat of conscription was looming, so I was starting to prepare for life with NORAD, the North American Aerospace Defense Command. You might be thinking by its name that NORAD had nothing to do with music. It turns out that the organization had an active music division, and I could apply for, and most likely get accepted into, that program as an arranger. The downside was that I would have to do this for four years, two more than were required of those on active military duty. But I had a fear of arms, and to this day have never even held any type of gun. (Okay, I had a water pistol and cap gun when I was five years old.)

As it turned out, I did not pass my physical exam when brought before the draft board, and this meant I could commence my first real job as assistant conductor in St. Louis. Prior to that, my interactions with composers were usually just limited to conversation, which was the case at both Juilliard and Aspen. Occasionally I would read through pieces by William Bolcom, Thomas Pasatieri, and Donald York, among others, but when I was studying conducting, my role as a creator was put on hold.

My composition aspirations returned in 1971, when I wrote a piece for St. Louis native Vincent Price. *The Raven* is a setting for narrator and orchestra of five poems by Edgar Allan Poe, and to this day is the longest piece I have ever written, coming in at slightly under a half hour. To my great surprise, Vincent was engaged by several other orchestras to perform the work, and other actors took it up as well. When I revisited the score in 2019 with the Manhattan School of Music, we performed and recorded the piece with Alec

Baldwin reciting the text. While admittedly derivative of so many other composers, the work has held up well, and the orchestration was sophisticated enough to make it interesting.

In the years since that first large-scale effort, I have written several occasional pieces, usually just for a singular event. It was not until 2014 that my compositional activity became more serious, with longer and more complex works. I wrote a piece for woodwind sextet and strings called *Endgames*, one dedicated to my mother and father—*Kinah*—as well as a work for the St. Louis Symphony Youth Orchestra, *Bachanalia*.

In my opinion, all musicians should try to write something. It does not matter if they have any training as a composer. The act of making something that did not exist before helps musicians better understand and appreciate the composers they play day in and day out. For example, one might write a cadenza for a concerto, a short work for a solo instrument, or a vocalise, without worrying about the quality or even about performing this potential masterpiece. This exercise in creativity enables musicians to empathize with the travails of all those composers whom they might take for granted. It certainly provides insight into the talent of the masters.

Many performers have the opportunity to work with a living composer. This interactive experience affords them a chance to ask questions and get clarification as to how the work is supposed to go. In many cases, they can assist in the creation itself by offering advice about what is possible to play and what is not. A solo instrumentalist or vocalist might confer with the composer throughout the creative process.

Most of the conductor's interactions with the composer take place during rehearsals, when the sound comes alive and it is easier to determine what works. My method for rehearsing with the composer present is to have the orchestra play through the new piece in its entirety during the first session. Then I ask the composer to bring me any changes or comments the next day, usually letting him or her address the orchestra directly to save time.

Part of the success of a new work depends on the level of respect the conductor has for the composer and vice versa. The more experienced composers know which interpreters to trust and which need guidance in bringing the piece to life. Ultimately, the job of the performer is to convey what the author wants. If, in the end, the conductor does not care for the piece, he or she should not let the orchestra, composer, or audience know.

Having performed so many pieces by living composers, and having worked closely with several, I can say that almost no one gets everything right. Remember my axiom, "The clock is the enemy of the conductor?" Think about how much rehearsal time goes into preparing a new work. Not only do the members of the orchestra need to learn the notes, they also have to correct mistakes in the parts, ask questions about dynamics, and deal with awkward page turns and mute changes.

Here are ten commandments I have devised for composers, designed to facilitate the rehearsal process and help move things along efficiently:

1. Please list all the instruments, including percussion, on the page just prior to the first page of music. Also indicate how many players are required to play the wind, brass, and percussion parts and who plays what. If you have questions, ask the players. This is particularly important in the case of percussion, but also applies to other instruments. For example, if you are writing for two flutes and piccolo, we need to know if the 2nd flute also plays its baby sister.

2. Put in the dynamic level at which you wish any given passage to start. Restate the dynamic even after a two-bar rest.

3. When you write a crescendo, we all need to know how loudly it will end. And, of course, the reverse is true for a diminuendo.

4. Sforzandos need to be understood in context. We can interpret them either as strong, or within the dynamic that is already being played. You have to tell us how loud or soft you would like the notes to be.

5. There are three ways to assign two-part divisi in the strings. The lines can be divided between the inside and outside musicians on a stand, the first stand can play the upper part with the second stand on the lower part and so on, or the

front half of the section can play the top part and the remainder the bottom part. Composers should figure this out
to save rehearsal time. It is helpful to keep in mind the seating of the orchestra for the first performance. These days,
several groups utilize the older system of placing the second
violins to the right of the conductor. Knowing this could
influence how you write for the totality of that instrumental
group.

6. For the brass, please indicate the type of mute you want
   them to use. Just writing *con sordino* does not work these
   days. There are many different options depending on the
   color you are looking for, so let us know.

7. In slow music, don't use a tempo that requires 64th and
   128th notes. It may look interesting in the score, but it
   causes the musicians to believe that they have to practice
   these passages quickly even if the metronome mark indicates
   otherwise.

8. Remember that the individual member of the orchestra
   only sees his or her part. Therefore, the occasional indication of what is happening prior to an entrance (a cue) helps.

9. Utilize measure numbers, but also letters or rehearsal numbers to indicate phrases or good starting points for the conductor. Imagine you are the cymbal player and there are
   only the measure numbers indicated in your parts. Perhaps
   eighty-five bars pass before you play, but the conductor
   might wish to start at bar 46. You might have difficulty figuring out where that is without the help of more frequent
   rehearsal letters and shorter multi-measure rests. And do not
   put in the additional indications arbitrarily every ten bars,
   for example, but rather place them where they make the
   most musical sense.

10. Finally, when you have completed writing your piece, print
    out the parts one by one and read through them yourself as
    if you were actually playing the part. This allows you to see
    the traps that I have laid out above and correct them, thus
    saving rehearsal time. Because of the technology available
    today, most new works have very few mistakes regarding

the notes. But still, even with good playback systems, some errors go undetected. Musicians will come up to the writer and me to point out something that does not seem correct. The composer often will say, "You are right, but the error was because of the computer program." None of us likes to hear that. It says to us that the author did not check everything.

If some of this seems cumbersome and laborious, it is all intended to make the rehearsal more focused on the music rather than whatever accidents could have been prevented in the first place. We are all there to help the composer achieve the results intended. It doesn't matter if the orchestra likes the piece or not. They are professionals and know their jobs. If the composer is satisfied, then we are. And for the week I spend rehearsing and performing the new work, I need to think it is the best piece I have ever conducted.

14

ON PERFORMANCE PRACTICE

Authenticity means erasing the gap between what you firmly believe inside and what you reveal to the outside world.

—Adam Grant

Important milestones change the way we think about music. Some cite the first performance of the "Eroica" Symphony as the watershed moment. Others believe that the premiere of *Le Sacre du printemps* was the turning point. The Beatles' first trip to the United States marked another such occasion. Perhaps forgotten in this mix is a recording that was released in October of 1968.

In keeping with the mind–altering state of hallucinogenic substances, *Switched-On Bach* became a smash hit and generated a lot of heated discussion. I was in my first year as assistant conductor in St. Louis and had already started doing a live radio show every Thursday. Since this program was meant to embrace all genres, I decided to play the whole album, without having heard a single track prior to the broadcast.

I loved it.

Rock and roll (where is the "roll" these days?) had embraced synthesizers, and electronic instruments were sneaking their way into jazz and other forms of music. Electronic experiments went back to the days preceding even the theremin. But Wendy Carlos had done something different, taking the notes Bach wrote and transforming them with a Moog synthesizer to embrace a whole new crowd.

Along the way, they heard the music of the Baroque master, but most people bought the record primarily for its sound quality.

For one of my early Sunday Festival of Music concerts in St. Louis, I invited Wendy to be a soloist. At this point, I did not know much about how the music would be played live. As it turned out, the performance hinged on a playback device and a keyboard. The soloist played only one line, which was supplemented by the pre-recorded tape and the orchestra. It appeared that this was more suited to the studio than the concert environment.

But time marched on. Or maybe it went backward.

During my school years, there was little or no talk of trying to replicate how musicians performed music when it was written. Rather, we inherited traditions that were passed on from teachers to students, who in turn would become the mentors for the next generation. There were always different schools of thought, be it Russian versus French pianism, Italian versus English singing, or any number of string methods. But one pattern was consistent: the musicians played in styles that moved the music forward.

Enter the period instrument movement. It is not clear when it actually began, but at least around the same time as synth Bach, we had the start of retro Bach. Meanwhile, attempts to duplicate, or at least bring to light, music prior to the Baroque era were underway. In particular, vocal works ranging all the way back to the days of Gregorian chant started to attract an audience. The harpsichord, given new life by Wanda Landowska, was becoming the instrument that would replace the piano in the performance of a great number of the early works. Countertenors were no longer the curiosity and sometimes chuckle-inducing anomaly they once were. Russell Oberlin and Alfred Deller led the way for many.

Gradually, the orchestral world started to pay attention. Specialist conductors and orchestras sprang up all over the world. Keep in mind that we were probably at the height of the recording industry, and we were starting to lose some of the greats who kept the companies in business. This is important because, as several commentators have pointed out, despite the claim that the historically informed movement was meant to replicate how music sounded in the past, it was very much a creation of the mid-20th century through the medium of sonic reproduction.

The research into historical performance practice was widespread. All of a sudden, those stodgy classes on species counterpoint and discussions of Johannes Ockeghem and Jacob Obrecht were becoming more relevant. But with the newfound discovery of what the past might have been about, we also wound up losing something valuable. Many orchestras found themselves struggling to figure out how to deal with a public expecting to hear music that sounded like these new chamber orchestra recordings. The large symphonic groups started dividing the orchestra into two separate ensembles, assigning half to Baroque or Classical repertoire and the other half to pops or children's concerts.

Most of the time, they simply played Haydn, Mozart, or Bach in the manner that existed in the first part of the 20th century. Understandably, no one was imposing the historically informed rules and regulations, as these performance techniques were not yet being taught. Groups like the Academy of St. Martin in the Fields, the English Chamber Orchestra, the Orchestra of St. Luke's, and the Saint Paul Chamber Orchestra held on to the traditions of the recent past. Meanwhile, specialists such as Christopher Hogwood, Sir Roger Norrington, and Trevor Pinnock were leading the charge to bring the treatises and tomes of the 18th century into practice.

The period performance conventions did not change my feelings about how I would choose to lead these works. And therein lay the real problem. We can look back at recordings of the Brandenburg concerti and find versions led by Reiner, or a Bach suite conducted by Toscanini, for example. When is the last time a label released a recording of Baroque music led by one of the music directors of a great orchestra? It just does not happen anymore. Conductors of conventional symphony orchestras have been shut out of a lot of this repertoire by the recording industry. One could easily add that at least in the States, it is fiscally irresponsible to program Bach, Handel, or Telemann with a small orchestra while still having to pay the full ensemble.

If any of us were to play this music the way we heard it when we were young, critics would put us in scorn's way. The contrast between imagining how music was played and how we might do it now has been a major issue of contention among musicians. I agree with Sir Neville Marriner, who famously said, "If Bach had a modern toilet, he would have used it." So we all have to ask ourselves an important question: With so many possibilities regarding how to play older music, how do we decide?

In 2020, the world celebrated the 250th anniversary of the birth of Beethoven—not that he needed the attention. Orchestras all over the place put on cycles of the symphonies, concerti, and anything they could find with his name on it. They even unearthed a couple scraps of paper with newly discovered music. So much for all the "complete" recorded editions of Ludwig's music that appeared during the past few decades.

Carnegie Hall got on the birthday bandwagon by presenting not one but two sets of performances of "The Nine." The first was by the period-instrument ensemble Orchestre Révolutionnaire et Romantique, under the direction of the orchestra's founder, Sir John Eliot Gardiner. In pre-concert interviews he made a point of saying that this was just another way of listening to the music and not a treatise on how the pieces should always be played. Fair enough.

The other cycle, postponed due to COVID-19, was with the Philadelphia Orchestra under Yannick Nézet-Séguin. The expectation was that this would be Beethoven as if Stokowski or Ormandy were leading the group. Unless Nézet-Séguin adopted any of the stylistic nuances of Gardiner, the contrast would have been interesting. Perhaps more intriguing would be a cycle in which the two interpretations are presented back-to-back so that the audience could immediately perceive the differences. We live comfortably with several different approaches, but it was disheartening to see a couple of critics write about the traditional, "stodgy" performances given by major orchestras.

Really? Perhaps there are still many listeners out there encountering the works for the first time. Or maybe the interpretations have something unique to say about the music. Just listen to the Sixth Symphony in recorded performances by Toscanini, Furtwängler, Karajan, or many of an endless list of those who have tackled the mountain. If one is bored by the traditional set of performance practices, it makes no sense to even comment on them or attend a presentation of these works.

The sheer act of trying to comprehend what Beethoven, or any composer for that matter, is hoping we understand is daunting enough. And each listener perceives the performance in a different way. Perhaps it is not just about hearing yet another rendition of the same work but also about understanding it through someone else's ears. As performers, we are mostly concerned about getting closer to an unknown truth, whether through our studies or practice methods. How an individual perceives this is something we cannot control or even fully grasp.

It is this very point that makes it difficult for me to wholeheartedly embrace period-performance practice. We may be able to replicate how the music might have sounded, although that involves speculation, but we certainly cannot hear the music with the same ears that attended the premiere. All of us experience the arts in relation to what we know today. Our aural sense takes in the past with the knowledge of things that have come after that time. We look at a Van Gogh with eyes that have seen the works of Picasso. Shakespeare changes because we have understood Albee.

Swiss conductor/violinist Etienne Abelin had some interesting observations as a performer:

> Having studied both "modern" and "performance practice" approaches, my impression is that it's less about rules and more about a basic grasp of principles of a language. Done well, performance practice inputs can, in my experience, help performances get more lively and, for example, enhance characters of dance and speech (well beyond Baroque repertoire). Many "modern" (West)-European orchestras have learned those basic performance practice-derived principles and have the agility to quite easily go back and forth between approaches. I wonder if that has been less the case elsewhere in the world so far?[1]

As far as I can tell, the orchestras that have embraced a duality of performing practices tend to be smaller ensembles. Once in a while, a major ensemble will venture into this territory, but it is usually with someone other than the music director. Most conductors have adopted a few of the principles of early performance practice, but these have more to do with favoring less vibrato once in a while or perhaps taking quicker tempi.

The stronger the conductor, the more insistent he or she will be when it comes to performance practice. Most orchestras, at least those at the very highest levels, have one general approach to the majority of the standard repertoire. They do not mind being challenged, particularly when a specialist is on the podium. Adapting to a different way of performance practice is becoming more normal for today's orchestras.

The problem arises when a visiting conductor leads a group that is steeped in the older style, but the guest is not comfortable with the way the ensemble plays this music. Having two different sets of opinions may seem interesting, but it really puts some roadblocks in the way of the singular journey. It would be impossible for me to play Gershwin, for example, in a manner that was heard in the 1920s. I do try to keep some of the rhythmic elements, but only in the context of how our orchestras perform today.

One of the givens once the piano was invented was that keyboardists could take on repertoire that had been written for the harpsichord. We still hear this today, especially with Bach. There was a story that went around many years ago. Pianist Rosalyn Tureck—with whom I worked a few times—met harpsichordist Wanda Landowska. After a few polite exchanges, Landowska reportedly said, "My dear, you can play Bach your way, and I will play it Bach's way."

Our society has made significant technological strides since Beethoven took a horse-drawn carriage to his own concert presentations. We no longer read the music by candlelight. Performance space for orchestras is at least twice the size as it was in Ludwig's time. Now, it is possible to read about the works prior to coming to a performance, not to mention listen to several versions on the internet. All of this, and more, influences our experience. It cannot be the same as it was.

15

ON REHEARSING

Practice makes perfect, but nobody's perfect, so why practice?

—Kurt Cobain

My father was a remarkable violinist, among other talents he possessed. Three or four weeks might have passed without him having touched the instrument, but then he could take it out of the case and launch right into the Tchaikovsky Concerto as if he had played it the night before. My mother, on the other hand, needed to have her cello in hand every day. In some ways, they were jealous of each other's study methods, because my father knew it should not come that easily, and my mom knew that there were other things she should be doing instead of practicing all the time.

For the conductor, studying is a very complicated matter. We do not have, nor do we want, a full orchestra in our living room. The budding podium-minder has no option but to sit alone, score on a table or the desk of the piano, and muddle through all those notes that are silently waiting on the page. It is a lonely business to glean knowledge in this solitary manner.

There is one, gigantic difference between the conductor's role in rehearsal and the instrumentalist's task during practice: our old friend the clock is ticking away for the one with the baton. Instrumentalists, whether student or professional, can practice for as long as they would like to. Several hours may pass before they move to the next item on their daily agenda. It is possible to practice nonstop or to take breaks at their discretion. The same freedoms only apply to conductors when they are engaging in score study.

Imagine that you are a conductor preparing for an upcoming concert opportunity. Eventually, the day of reckoning arrives, and your first rehearsal with the orchestra looms large. Keep in mind that until this point, very few time constraints have been placed on your learning process. Now, however, there is a finite amount of time in which you must accomplish all that you feel needs to be done. What might have taken hours to learn is reduced to minutes and seconds during rehearsal. Time management is something that cannot be practiced at home. You have to learn it on the spot.

Let's look at an average week for an orchestra. The rehearsal and performance periods are called services. Professional orchestras usually schedule between seven and nine of these per week. The number depends on the total for the entire season, with some weeks shortened or lengthened depending on what occurred in the previous week. Rarely can there be nine services for more than two weeks in a row, and musicians are entitled to a certain number of days off in between the end of one service week and the beginning of the next. This is all carefully monitored by the operations and personnel managers.

Let's assume that you will have four rehearsals for your program, which will include a world premiere, a concerto, and a work from the standard canon. The first order of business is to construct a program that is within the parameters of the rehearsal time and possible to accomplish adequately in four periods. This is not as easy as you might think.

For the purpose of this exercise, we will assume you are conducting an orchestra somewhere in the United States. Let's call it the Six Rivers Philharmonic, and let's presume that it has seventy-five musicians on the roster. Your program should not utilize more players, as hiring extra musicians has an impact on the orchestra's budget. The musicians will play this concert two times during the week, utilizing a total of six services. Perhaps any remaining services in that week are given to educational concerts, readings of young composers' works, or a pops program in between the two concerts that you are conducting.

The world premiere is a ten-minute piece by the orchestra's composer in residence. Unfortunately, the work was not completed until just a few weeks ago, so you did not know the degree of difficulty or challenge to the orchestra it would pose. When the score arrives, you can see that the strings play a lot of notes in a work called *Rondo Furioso*. In addition, the piece includes unanticipated special effects that will require lengthy explanations to the orchestra.

The composer had told you about a year ago that the piece was going to be an elegy, which led you to believe the work would be rather slow and uncomplicated. So you decided to program Korngold's Symphony in F-sharp on the second half. This rather difficult and dense piece is quite a rarity and completely unknown to the orchestra, not to mention the audience. Thankfully the Tchaikovsky First Piano Concerto, the vehicle of choice for the soloist, would boost ticket sales. Now that you realize the world premiere will take more time than anticipated, you have to rethink your rehearsal plan.

Most orchestras ask you to communicate the rehearsal schedule about two months in advance, not only the order of pieces to be rehearsed, but also how much time you expect to spend on each one. And even though it may not be required in the collective bargaining agreement with the musicians, the preference is to do the works in descending order by orchestral size, meaning that you begin the day with the largest orchestra and end with a piece requiring fewer players.

You have one rehearsal on Tuesday. This will be two-and-a-half hours long with a twenty-minute break. There is no need to rehearse the Tchaikovsky, as the soloist will not be in town yet and the orchestra played the work a couple of years ago. Your main decision is to figure out if you want to begin with the Korngold or the new piece. The former exists in a musical idiom familiar to most musicians, even though the piece is new to the orchestra. The new, complicated work will require the musicians to not only learn the notes but also master a few new techniques employed by the composer.

How does the first rehearsal commence? Conductor Tim Franklin reminded me of a different time:

> There is a frequently shared story that for many years Dr. James Croft, Director of Bands at Florida State University, would

begin rehearsals with the graduate wind ensemble by stepping off the podium. At that point, every musician would stand and bow slightly. This was in recognition that everyone was remembering that they were in service to the music, and equally important, in service to each other. It was also noted that in no way were they bowing to an authoritarian leader on the podium.[1]

Probably it is best to start with the Korngold, since you will not have to talk so much and can digest how well the musicians are coping with the piece. Spend about an hour and fifteen minutes on it, rehearsing for a short while after the initial play-through. Go through the fast and note-filled sections at a slower tempo so the musicians can get an idea as to what they will need to practice individually. The contract specifies that you must take a break before the hour-and-a-half point. The percussion has to be reset, and this can occur during the twenty minutes between the two halves of the rehearsal.

You now have around fifty minutes to process the *Rondo*. It looks difficult because of all the notes, so rather than an in-tempo run-through, you should more than likely rehearse at a slower speed with dynamics on the softer side, as you did in the Korngold—just enough to show the musicians what difficulties lie ahead. Oh, I forgot to mention that several of the players did not take the music home in advance to practice on their own. So you are the person who will teach this piece to them, right from the first beat.

After the somewhat lethargic play-through, and with a lot of confused faces in the orchestra, you begin at the beginning, in the tempo specified by the composer, but you stop as needed to go over passages that were played incorrectly. The composer is there, mostly to help but also to listen, deciding what works and what does not. She will take copious notes and, by the next day, will make several alterations to accidentals and dynamics, make cuts, or even add some music. Everyone has to be prepared for changes.

This session ends at the appointed two and a half hours. The rest of your day will be spent going over what occurred during the rehearsal and deciding how you will handle tomorrow's gatherings of the musical forces, morning and afternoon. Having a game plan for rehearsals is really important, as you do not want to fall behind prior to the dress rehearsal. In effect, it is this second day when much of the detailed work will be done. Think about what did not work in the Korngold, whether it was a misjudgment on your part or something the orchestra might have misconstrued. Always assume that everything that doesn't go well is your fault, and if you later decide that you did a certain part well, then you can assign responsibility elsewhere. Usually it is a matter of playing a passage a couple of times to achieve the clarity you desire.

Day Two begins with a timetable similar to the one employed during the first rehearsal. I would start with the new piece and give it an hour and fifteen minutes. Begin at the spot where you left off the day before and work through to the end. Then play the piece through completely so that you, the orchestra, and the composer get comfortable with the entire work. If there is time left, you might want to clean up a few passages before the clock runs out. Have no doubt, if you cannot see the timepiece, the personnel manager will pop onstage a couple of minutes before the buzzer.

After the twenty-minute break, go to the Korngold and start at the beginning, reminding the orchestra of what they worked on previously, and then continue to rehearse as much of the rest of the piece as you can. The lunch break is either an hour or an hour and a half. During this time, you meet with the soloist, who has been practicing in one of the rooms nearby. If it is an artist you know, all you need to discuss are those passages that present coordination difficulties. More importantly, try to get a feeling for what the pianist is doing musically, so that you can match phrases that are duplicated in the orchestra. Often, however, what you and the soloist discuss may not be the same as what occurs onstage later that afternoon. Acoustics, nerves, and the responsiveness of the keyboard are just a few of the factors that come into play and cannot be judged in advance. Overall, spontaneity is a positive aspect of collaborating with a soloist.

After the break, continue with the Korngold until you are confident that the musicians are comfortable in their knowledge of the piece. A two-hour rehearsal usually has a fifteen-minute intermission, so in reality, there is just an hour and three-quarters of actual music-making. If you use an hour for the symphony, you will have forty-five minutes left for the concerto, which takes thirty-five to play through. If you stick to this plan, only ten minutes will remain to actually rehearse passages. More than likely, your best bet is to wrap up the Korngold in forty-five minutes, and then you have an hour for the Tchaikovsky.

The piano was put onstage during the pause, so you do not have to worry about that. You introduce the soloist to the orchestra, and everyone is ready to begin. Since the work is familiar, my advice is to play through the first movement, minus the several cadenzas, and then go back to fix any problems that occurred. If you are fortunate to have an assistant or cover conductor, he or she can help solve any balance issues. Do this for each movement and end the rehearsal.

Next, you have to think about what to do for the dress rehearsal. Usually, this is just a run-through of the program in order. Remember what I said about working from large orchestra to small? For this rehearsal, you can usually bend that rule and perform all of the works in concert order. That way, everyone gets the feel for the overall arc of the program, the stagehands get a test-run of the setup changes in between pieces, and you have an opportunity to gauge how physically demanding the program will be. After running through each piece, address any details that did not go as you wished, and then bid the orchestra farewell until the concert.

Former National Symphony Orchestra violinist Paula Akbar succinctly summarized the overall challenge of the rehearsal process and her ideal method, with which I happen to agree:

> As every musician is different and learns in different ways, there will be as many different rehearsal preferences as there are musicians. As a big-picture person, my own preference is to scope out the whole and work inward to details.[2]

Of course, different programs make for different rehearsal plans. But the outline I have provided is a basic work ethic that can be adjusted to each situation. Do not propose programs that cannot be accomplished in the time allotted for rehearsal. Limit your talking to just what the orchestra needs. Imagine that you are playing in the ensemble. What would you want to hear from the conductor? And if by the time you have concluded your rehearsals you are still worried about the concert, then it is time to pray.

IV

FOURTH MOVEMENT

16

ON AUDIENCES

With public sentiment, nothing can fail. Without it, nothing can succeed.

—Abraham Lincoln

It is about a half hour prior to the start of the concert. The ushering staff has had a confab and has been given last minute instructions for the event. When are the latecomers seated? Will I need to use my flashlight? What is the difference between the dress circle and the lower balcony? Where is row FF?

Anxiously waiting in the lobby are several hundred concertgoers, hoping to get to their seats early enough to read the program book. Others are in the donor lounge, eating and drinking, generally looking forward to the performance. And some are still trying to find a parking spot, hoping not to miss the downbeat.

There is also a small group of patrons wondering how long the contemporary piece at the start of the concert will last. Conceivably, if they reviewed the program online, they realized that they could arrive ten minutes late to avoid the anticipated dissonance and settle in comfortably with the Tchaikovsky concerto that follows. Perhaps the concerto is the only piece they want to hear, and they will depart the venue at intermission.

The appointed hour has arrived, and everyone is waiting for the inevitable Voice of God announcement informing them of all the things they cannot do. No pictures. No recording devices. Silence all cell phones. Please fasten your seat belts. After acknowledgement of the people and corporations lending fiscal support for the concert, the words, "Enjoy the concert" are intoned, and the performance begins.

But wait! Why did this occur around five minutes after the scheduled start time? Many orchestras have a built-in hold at the beginning of a concert. To help ensure a full concert experience for the few people who arrive just a bit late, the musicians' contract specifies that the orchestra should begin their part of the bargain a little later than the start time announced to the public. Supposedly this helps prevent an overtime situation at the end of the concert. However, some audience members have figured this out and know that they are safe if they delay their arrival to the hall by a few minutes.

What they do not know is how long a concert is officially supposed to last, according to the guidelines outlined in the collective bargaining agreement. Usually, the standard is a maximum performance time of no more than two hours and fifteen minutes, beginning at the agreed-upon start time and lasting until the moment the concertmaster leaves the stage.

Now that we know when the concert starts and ends, you would think that everything is pretty clear cut. Such is not the case. Extraneous matters can alter the plan dramatically, and the people in attendance become unknowing participants in a complex set of regulations. For example, the clock begins ticking at the contractual start time, even if the actual start time of the program is delayed due to unforeseen circumstances. Also, I cannot count the number of occasions on which I have been sent onto the stage to begin the second half of the concert, only to have to wait for the stragglers to get settled. There are few annoyances worse than having to watch audience members barrel their way over others who then have to stand up and allow them in. (Why does it seem that the last people to arrive are always in the first two rows?)

Then there is the really unfortunate rule regarding when a concert concludes. You would think that the logical end time corresponds with the last sound produced by the musicians. After all, the orchestra has performed its function and is at that point receiving well-deserved recognition from the audience. But no, until the concertmaster leaves his or her chair, the clock is still ticking. And here is where we get to a major dilemma faced by conductors and orchestra managers.

As musicians, we serve several masters. First and foremost is the composer. Next are the members of the orchestra. Then come our supporters, both those who attend the concerts as well as the people who make it financially possible for us to do our jobs. We are also indebted to the communities where we work and are tasked with trying to inspire as many people as possible through great music, no matter the genre. We cannot afford to alienate any of these constituents. With that in mind, here is the problem:

Suppose a concert contains around an hour and forty-five minutes of music. That is the average program length, assuming the tried-and-true format of an opening piece followed by a concerto and then a symphony. If we are playing a ten-minute contemporary piece, this might be preceded by a short set of introductory comments by the composer or conductor. Perhaps the next piece is a Chopin piano concerto. If the piano is not in place during the first piece on the program, it will take around five minutes for the instrument to be wheeled in from an offstage position or, more dramatically, lifted from the bowels below the stage.

After three curtain calls, the soloist may choose to play an encore or two. These can range from two to ten minutes. With applause, we now have a first half that comprises an hour of music, stage changes, and audience response. Intermission times vary but are usually fifteen to twenty minutes long, depending not on the audience but rather on what the contract with the musicians stipulates. We are now an hour and twenty minutes into the evening, leaving us with fifty-five minutes for the second half.

At this point, the orchestra staff is looking at that dreaded clock, comparing the anticipated runtime with the number of minutes left before overtime payments kick in. A standard work, such as a Brahms or Beethoven symphony, comes in at forty to forty-five minutes. But there are variables, including which repeats a conductor chooses to take, or the tempi that define this performance.

It all seems fine on paper, but then comes the unexpected. It could be waiting for latecomers in the audience, or perhaps one musician has not made it to the stage yet. Maybe the tuning process takes a bit longer than expected, or the conductor is slow to enter. Meanwhile, the clock is winding down.

At last, the music comes to an end. What a performance! The ovation is tremendous. After recognizing individual members of the orchestra for their solo contributions, an overly satisfied conductor walks to the door, eagerly awaiting a return to the stage for further bows and adulation. But guess what? The second hand is fast approaching the dreaded moment of overtime. The orchestra has to be told to get off the stage, thereby denying the audience members the opportunity to show their full appreciation. The stage manager signals the concertmaster, who then gets up and leaves, orchestra in tow. On tour—and this has happened to me several times—it can mean depriving the public of an encore or two, which in some cases can be the highlight of a program.

I realize that this may seem petty, but the race against the clock is something that weighs heavily on many of us who lead the performances, presenting added pressure to control all the variables, some of which are unpredictable. In the context of a performance, the countdown does little to serve musical principles. The abrupt cutoff can be insulting to the audience or embarrassing to the members of the orchestra when it affects the length of time available for applause.

The solution is simple. Since most rehearsals are two-and-a-half hours long, why can't the concert be the same length? When we do the dress rehearsal, we are, in effect, going through the show in concert order, exactly as it will be heard either that night or the next day. Most conductors try to keep the program length at two hours or so, but on the rare occasion that the concert exceeds that time-frame, this is when the worry sets in. Let's relieve the tension, favor our audience, and change the concert-length allowance. Moreover, the public's response at the end of the concert should not be part of the time allotted to the length of the performance. Rather, it should be acknowledged as an opportunity for an exchange of appreciation between orchestra and audience.

By the way, who truly constitutes what is called "The Audience"? *Merriam-Webster* is quite clear about the definition: "a group of listeners or spectators." There is no mention of whether or not they are actually in attendance at the venue. In fact, this gathering of souls can be watching the performance from a bar, listening on the car radio, or connecting with the event online. This last method of tuning in was very important to the well-being of the Detroit Symphony Orchestra (DSO) following its devastating strike in 2010–2011.

An allowance in the contract that settled the strike made it possible for the orchestra to livestream the video of each of its classical subscription programs at no cost to the consumer and no payment to the musicians beyond the electronic media guarantee that was part of their overall compensation. As of this writing, no other orchestra in the United States has been able to do anything similar due to the restrictions set up in an outdated agreement with the musicians' union. COVID-19 changed the pattern as organizations sought new ways to connect with audiences during the outbreak.

In Detroit, we were able to secure foundation money that would cover the costs of stagehands, technical crew, and other staff involved in the effort behind the scenes. These people were the ones who had to make changes or add to the workload they already had to make the webcasts possible. At first, our offerings were clumsy and awkward. Over the years, the rapid development of robotic cameras and high-end audio equipment afforded us an opportunity to create very sophisticated broadcasts. Originally just airing live on the day of the concert, the project blossomed into one that included an on-demand video streaming archive. For a fifty-dollar donation to the orchestra's annual fund, the viewer could watch any concert going back thirty-six months. During my time with the DSO, I am aware of only one soloist or conductor who refused to participate in the webcast, and that decision was dictated by his record company.

In addition to the weekly webcasts, I had an idea about livestreaming a full DSO rehearsal, with the intent of showing young conductors, as well as the general public, what goes into putting a concert together. Unfortunately, the musicians' union denied the proposal. The federation's rules limited me to fifteen minutes of audiovisual capture, and even though we did broadcast this sneak peek at the rehearsal process, it was of little value due to the restricted timeframe. An educational opportunity was wasted because no one would get paid for something they were already doing for a salary.

The pop music field has had the right idea for a long time. Make the recording, then release the video and use it to promote the concert tour. Why can't orchestras do the same? Broadcast the concert, build up the audience base online, then find ways to entice fans to the live event, where the remote viewers would turn into paying customers. Pretty simple.

If we are to grow our listenership, it is crucial to adjust to the times in which we live. YouTube can only go so far. It is up to the individual cultural institutions to find the means by which to attract the audience. And it behooves the unions not only to look after the financial interests of their membership but also to help orchestras and individuals reach the most people possible with whatever tools they have in their collective bargaining workshop.

In this installment, I have tried to look at two ways we deal with the audience. One seems an occasional irritation, albeit one that can negatively impact the audience, and the other is wide-ranging in terms of making music accessible to more listeners and viewers. Both are meant to remind everyone that those who support our cultural institutions must always be taken into equal consideration with the performers when it comes to the full representation of our product. Without an audience, we exist in a vacuum. And—well, you all know the expression.

17

ON FORGOTTEN MASTERS

I like the dreams of the future better than the history of the past.

—Thomas Jefferson

I have changed my place of residence too many times to remember. When I returned to St. Louis in 2018 following my departure as music director in Detroit, the move was a matter of practicality. My wife and I had scouted out several possibilities around the country, but with friends in St. Louis, not to mention its outstanding medical facilities, the ease of getting around, and my favorite baseball team, I felt like I was coming home.

Part of any relocation is figuring out what to keep from the former home and what to discard. There was little time to sort everything out, and I knew that most of the weeding would be done when the big truck arrived, loaded with many relics of the past. I was still recuperating from triple bypass, so enlisting the aid of my son and his fiancée made the task easier.

The possessions to be divvied up fell into three main categories: recorded material in the form of LPs, CDs, and the like; books; and an extensive library of printed music. For more than forty years, my scores had been stored with the orchestras that I led. Each archive had cataloged my collection in different ways. Now I was the head librarian, and that meant it was time to see what had accumulated as well as what should be discarded. Oh, we had to convert one of the bedrooms into a *bibliothèque*.

We encountered orchestral scores, piano music, my father's violin music from when he was a student at the Curtis Institute, jazz and pop charts, and the occasional piece that I could not categorize. Dividing them up alphabetically made the most sense, but I needed to adjust some of the lower shelves to allow for the oversized scores that could not fit into the normal spaces.

As we systematically went through the composers, it became evident that a large portion of my collection consisted of composers and pieces that many conductors working today would not recognize. I own complete sets of symphonies by William Schuman and Walter Piston, for example. Scores by Roger Sessions, Roy Harris, Howard Hanson, David Diamond, Vincent Persichetti, Peter Mennin, and so many others brought back a flood of memories.

Had I conducted all the works in my stockpile? No, I would not have had the time to do anything like that. However, none of the scores had gone unopened and, in several cases, I had made annotations, which indicated that some form of study of the unperformed pieces had taken place. These included Mendelssohn's *Elijah,* Bruckner's Ninth Symphony, and several works by Bach. Yes, I had conducted all the orchestral music by Brahms, but even the *Deutsches Requiem* had to wait until I was in my sixties to receive a first performance on my part.

As I put the scores on the racks, my mind kept returning to those great symphonists from the middle of the 20th century. This was the time when Americans made their boldest statements in a form that was decidedly European. We were a little bit late to the party, seeing as though the Germans and Austrians had abandoned these structural schemes earlier in the century. Only the English and Russians hung on, from Vaughan Williams to Shostakovich. Today the symphony as a formal architectural plan has changed, and arguably has almost disappeared.

Consider those Americans I listed a few paragraphs earlier. Their output comprises ten symphonies by Schuman (two unpublished), eight by Piston, eight by Sessions, sixteen by Harris, seven by Hanson, eleven by Diamond, nine by Persichetti, and nine by Mennin. Are these symphonies all masterpieces? Certainly not, but even their best works are not encountered often in the concert hall these days.

To generations of both musicians and listeners that did not grow up with these names, they seem to be outdated and old-fashioned.

Every country can say the same thing. Whatever happened to Nikolai Myaskovsky, who wrote twenty-seven symphonies, or Havergal Brian, who churned out thirty-two of them? It is certainly possible to argue that the last work in that form to enter the canon of pieces played on a regular basis was the Tenth Symphony of Shosta-kovich. And that was back in 1953!

As the trip down memory lane in my library continued, another question began to arise. What happened to the generation following those symphonic giants in the States? Once again, I found a myriad of works that I had conducted, many of which were premieres, by composers that have fallen off the radar. Once-familiar voices are now mostly absent from our concert halls. Jacob Druckman, Don-ald Erb, Michael Colgrass, Leon Kirchner, William Bergsma, Ned Rorem, Alan Hovhaness, among others, were lauded and performed often during their lifetimes.

Is there a generational divide when it comes to modern music? It seems as if fame is only acknowledged during the lifetime of the contemporary composer. Perhaps this can be partially attributed to the fact that conductors and presenters enjoy giving premieres. Con-sider this: Pierre Boulez and Elliott Carter, both of whom made an undeniable imprint on the musical landscape, have seemingly been left on the scrapheap of history when it comes to performances of their orchestral scores. It is almost impossible to find record of any performances of their music, other than their solo or chamber works, in America since their passing.

In his book *Raymond Leppard on Music*, the conductor wrote:

High art will never be really easy of access, but it must have an element, a degree of initial communication involving the listener or else we shall not find our way to it. No longer does it count to say 'a time will come.' If we do not manage it in our time it seems no longer much comfort to say our children's children will understand.[1]

Indeed, I have been proud to champion living composers, some of whom have made important and lasting contributions. Much of my career was built on the presentation of contemporary works, with very few programs devoid of something new. And I did not promote American composers exclusively. If I encountered a work that really grabbed me, I would at least submit it to orchestras for their consideration. This was usually accepted, but often only if I was bringing an American work or something by a composer from the country in which I would be performing.

One of the questions that I am frequently asked by young conductors is, "What can I do to get my career started?" There is no single answer, but one of them has to do with choosing some part of the repertoire that few are actually performing these days. A creative project might garner attention and put the conductor on the map. For example, in 2009 most of the world ignored the 200th anniversary of the death of Haydn. During a visit to Indiana University that year, I suggested that the conducting class collaborate with some of their music-performance cohorts to play through all of that composer's symphonies. There are somewhere between 104 and 107 of them. It could be done within the course of the school year. With some promotional push behind it, the endeavor could pique the interest of the press, and that is one way for burgeoning conductors to get noticed.

Notably, when I spoke to those young conductors about the composers I mentioned early in this chapter, very few knew of them or their work. Part of keeping the arts alive means not only invigorating the canon with new works but also discovering what came before. In addition to the standard repertoire, which, unless one is a specialist, makes up the majority of the maestro's catalog, it is essential to find those pieces that can become signature works. My advice to aspiring conductors is to be bold and individual. The conductor's job is to entertain and enlighten.

Meanwhile, back to the library. I had no use for my father's violin music, so I sent it to Curtis, as it could be instructive for faculty and violinists to see the markings of my dad's teacher, Efrem Zimbalist. I shipped the jazz and pop charts, as well as other piano music, to my son, who is a film composer and could use these for reference. The fate of the recorded material, whether video or audio, depended on what I might ever watch or listen to again. This was slightly mitigated by a radio series I was beginning.

I have uploaded much of my audio collection onto my iPad. Sometimes on long flights, I put the device on shuffle mode, just for variety. The results are often fascinating. Not knowing what is coming next, whether folk, blues, comedy, jazz, or classical, keeps me interested for a couple of hours. That is the idea behind *The Slatkin Shuffle*, a weekly program on Classic 107.3 FM: The Voice for the Arts in St. Louis, and also available online. In determining what to cull from my library, I had to take the radio show into consideration, as the playlists need to include an unusual mix. For that reason, *The Legend Lives Forever in Latin*, a selection of Elvis Presley songs sung in the ancient language, did not go into the "away" box.

Finally, the toughest set of choices: Which scores should I keep, and which should go to the Manhattan School of Music, where I have been doing some conducting and teaching for the past six years? Although it was, at one time, instructive to have five different editions of all nine Beethoven symphonies, I certainly did not need them any longer. For the standard repertoire, I had already transferred a minimal number of annotations to the scores I actually use, and this held true for lesser-known works as well. I also eliminated virtually complete sets of music by Dvořák, Sibelius, Walton, and others. Rarely did I conduct from these, so again, having already added my own markings to another edition, out they went. I kept only those volumes that conceivably might appear in future programs.

The most difficult decisions had to do with all those composers I mentioned at the start of this chapter. Many of the scores had inscriptions from the authors. Others were reminders of a time when this music was a vital part of musical life for me. Some were sent by publishers for my perusal.

My collection also included pieces by students of my composer friends. In recent years, I have sought out works of the next generation. In fact, I commissioned six new pieces by young composers in my final season as music director in Detroit. In the compositions of these terrific new voices, one can see the influence of their esteemed instructors. This is the sense of musical continuity that defines the creative art. Watching composers grow and flourish is eminently satisfying. Perhaps someday, when my entire library finds another home, an enterprising young conductor will discover something and find that path to the past. The collection certainly includes treasures that should not go silent.

As for me, I am not sure if some of the scribblings in those manuscripts should remain. While nothing is offensive, the naiveté shown in some cases is a little embarrassing. No, we should leave behind what we thought in the hope that others will learn from our errors.

18

ON SOUND HEALTH

The world is noisy and messy. You need to deal with
the noise and uncertainty.

—Daphne Koller

Have you gone to the movies lately, especially to see one of those
action films with characters out of the world of comic books?
If the theater is state of the art, then we should consider moving
to another state. The advertising pitch prior to the feature proudly
proclaims how modern and up-to-date the sound system is. It could
be Dolby Atmos or DTS:X; any of the new technologies will do.
We all know that there will be loud moments, but still, we are not
informed as to the dangers of high decibel counts.

In that respect, I am just like most people. I get a certain thrill
from excessive decibel levels in theaters. But I dislike experiencing
the loud sounds of everyday life—walking by a street being pummeled by a jackhammer, hearing the agonizing cry of the police siren
as a car whizzes by, and even experiencing the sudden bang of the
airplane's overhead storage bin as it is slammed shut.

How well I remember my son's first reaction to the sound of
40,000 people at a baseball game. He was only three years old, and
the exuberant crowd was just too much for the little guy. This carried over to the amplified music that was played in the ice hockey
arena, which was far more aggressive than the actual sound of players
flying into the boards.

I suppose we can put the blame for loud sounds on Thomas Edison and Guglielmo Marconi. Their visionary inventions changed the way we hear the world. Even Henry Ford has to be held accountable. It had to be difficult working eight to ten hours on those first assembly lines amid constant hammering and pounding. Back then, there were not studies to alert people to the damage their eardrums were suffering.

My generation was the first to really experience the impact of large-scale amplification. Prior to the Sixties, there were microphones and so-called loudspeakers, but for the most part, the noise levels were not overwhelming. Parents decried them anyway, always with the same argument: "It wasn't that way when I was your age." In the home, we could enjoy broadcasts and recordings by the greatest of artists, but we were in control of the volume.

I do not remember anyone complaining about what it was like to sit onstage, directly in front of the trumpets or drums. It was part of orchestral life, and even though the sound produced was not that much different than today, no one said anything, probably for fear of losing his or her job. The same was true of other physical discomforts that went unspoken at the time, like carpal tunnel syndrome, loss of feeling in an arm, or muscle weakness throughout the body. These just came with the territory.

For about the past twenty-five years, we have seen studies that show the effects that years of toil can have on musicians. And for most of that time, various devices, some medical, have been utilized to help offset these ailments. If you have been to an orchestral concert, more than likely you have seen a few of these onstage. The most common, and most distracting, are plexiglass sound shields, which are placed in back of the musicians to reduce the volume coming from behind them. These are fairly large and unwieldy chunks of plastic that produce a glare and often a physical reflection that is visible to the audience.

The players believe that these screens deflect the sound away from their ears. While that may be true for those sitting in front of the shield, the overall effects are more complicated. Think about it from the point of view of the person who is playing into that shield. If it is a trumpet player, his or her sound is bouncing back, literally, thereby increasing the decibel level and sometimes, depending on the angle of the screen, producing an audible double sound of a single note. Not only that, but the barrier also alters the overall balance of sound that reaches into the auditorium. And it looks terrible.

Sometimes I spot a musician covering his or her ears when a very loud passage occurs. One would think that a professional percussionist might expect severe sound levels, yet time and time again, I have seen those very players who can make the most noise wince as their colleagues thwack away during *Le Sacre du printemps*. More than one composer has written a piece that calls for volume levels so extreme that orchestras have refused to play it.

One relatively effective solution is the use of a device that attaches to the back of the musician's chair. An absorbing cushion surrounds the lower portion of the head without actually touching the player's ears. It is certainly a more discreet way of preventing the sound waves from getting into the ear canal, but sadly, this has not really caught on. Perhaps we are not quite there with the onstage technology for volume protection, or maybe the psychological effects of the large plexiglass screen make it seem more useful, just because it is big.

Ear plugs are a widely used remedy. Some are designed specifically for musicians and come in various colors and materials. The best of them help to eliminate the extreme high and low frequencies that are the cause of so many problems. But they do make it more difficult to balance individual parts within the ensemble.

Recently, a member of the Nashville Symphony Orchestra announced that after quite a long time in the group, she and her husband were leaving. The two reasons stated were that they did not care for the direction of the programming, and they objected to the sheer volume of sound that they encountered, particularly during pops concerts. Is this the new reality in orchestral performance? What do the audiences make of the increased dynamic levels? Do we truly play louder now than we did a hundred years ago?

Before I address these issues, it is worth noting that when I was assistant conductor in St. Louis, the music director had programmed the Five Movements for String Orchestra by Anton Webern. I watched as two people left their seats during the third of these miniatures, which are mostly very soft in texture. Audibly, one said: "If he didn't want us to hear it, why did he write it?" It begs the question of dynamic levels used by composers since Giovanni Gabrieli. How soft is soft, and how loud is loud? Should there be limits on both the lower and upper ends of the dynamic range?

My own experience comes from being a listener as well as a participant. I played in orchestras as a violist when I was young, and I was also a pianist, operating as both a soloist and a member of the group. When I played the piano in the orchestra, I was usually positioned somewhere near the harp and percussion. This was mostly during the Sixties, and the repertoire I played was usually within the standard range of the listening spectrum. At the same time, I was going to rock concerts, jazz clubs, and yes, even discos, although more for the social experience rather than my ability to dance.

The jazz scene was usually acoustic, so even if one was seated near the drum kit, the sound was never overbearing. Sometimes, if it was a big band in a small venue, the volume seemed slightly excessive, but this was jazz, and I was not going to be deprived of hearing what was being produced. Rock concerts were another matter. When I arrived in St. Louis, I was in charge of programming the nonclassical events at a series known as the Mississippi River Festival. Being comfortable with and surprisingly knowledgeable in the field, I got to hang out with the musicians, learning a great deal about how they contended with the high decibel levels onstage.

Most of them simply said that they got used to it. Of course in some cases, a little toke of weed or swig of bourbon seemed to go a long way. No one ever spoke of the long-term effects like potential hearing loss. Over the years, I would encounter a couple of these musicians once in a while. Most of them seemed unchanged in their ability to hear. I am reminded of that great scene in *This Is Spinal Tap* in which one of the musicians says the band plays at a volume level of eleven ("one louder" than ten) but fails to understand the insignificance of the custom-printed number on the dial in terms of the amplifier's maximum output.

As for the club scene, I was a part of it only during my student years in New York. There were a seemingly endless variety of these venues, mostly for a far hipper set of kids. But I knew some people who got me in, and I went to try to figure out what the attraction was. Most certainly it was not for the purpose of conversation, as it was (and still is today) not really possible to hear over the din coming from the loudspeakers. My eventual conclusion was that the social convention of the time was to seek a natural or supplemented high from the experience. It was about the social order of things, not really the music. No one who goes to a club ever complains about how loud it is.

Let's get back to the Nashville musicians. In order to properly comprehend their decision, we need to understand the evolution of amplified sound in the concert hall. As the venues became larger, orchestras increased the number of players in the group. In turn, composers were, from the 20th century onward, writing for larger forces, especially in the percussion section. New instruments were being invented and developed, taking up even more space on the concert platform. Still, for the most part, amplification was not utilized for the symphonic canon. Only when the occasional pop act came in for a special concert did microphones begin to appear on a more regular basis.

Electronic music itself was a product of the Sixties. The people writing for orchestra were now starting to combine these new sounds with the orchestral sonorities, and this led to some of the traditional instruments becoming amplified. Enter the world of rock and the idea that a new audience could be attracted if these acts could appear with orchestra. I conducted the first live performance of *Jesus Christ Superstar*, and we sold out two performances in less than three hours. Metallica, one of the greatest and loudest bands in the country, made a splash when they appeared with the San Francisco Symphony. The rush was on to figure out other ways to cash in on a newfound market.

The bands usually brought in their own sound systems, much more sophisticated than anything available to orchestras. In turn, the volume was much louder than expected. The reason, in most cases, was simple. The rock groups were used to performing in stadiums, and the relative size of the concert hall was just not appropriate for the level of sound that was being produced. But the younger crowds loved it, and gradually, even a solo vocalist might jack up the sound in addition to amplifying the orchestral instruments.

Former Minnesota Orchestra cellist Janet Horvath, now an advocate for auditory protection, shared this explanation of the way the ear responds to sound exposure in a 2015 article published in the *Atlantic*:

> The ear has 20,000–30,000 hair cells, the nerve endings responsible for carrying the electrical impulses through the auditory nerve to the brain. These delicate receptors bend or flatten as sounds enter the ear, typically springing back to normal in a few hours, or overnight. But over time, loud sounds can cause more permanent damage as hair cells lose their resilience. Frequent and intense exposure to noise will cause these receptors to flatten down, stiffen, and eventually break. The damage can interfere with the ability to determine the location of a sound, cause extreme sensitivity and pain, and make it impossible to discern language with background noise. One in 20 Americans, or 48 million people, report some degree of hearing impairment.[1]

This brings up a dilemma for us musicians. If we are conscious of the perils of repeated exposure to high decibels, why pursue this profession in the first place? Are we not supposed to place our health at the front of the list when considering what to do? Maybe if we are aware that this is a calling, we have to put up with the potential for damage and just take it in stride. Someone entering competitive sports certainly understands what is at stake. Injury is an accepted part of those professions. Perhaps it is the same in orchestras. The passion for the music takes precedence, and often, health concerns do not enter into the picture for performers.

For some, including our friends in Music City, the noise became too much. This was not what they expected when they first embarked on their journey into the orchestral world. Few know what to anticipate when they enter the all-too-real world of high-level performance. In many ways, I wish that our music education institutions would address this early on. Why not have a concert or two during this formative time in a young musician's training in which they are exposed to what it will really be like when they enter the orchestral workforce? It could be a life-changing experience, either positive or negative, but at least it would reflect the reality of what to expect when entering the professional workplace.

These days there are numerous hearing devices available to help musicians cope with not only volume but frequency range as well. However, they can be costly. I believe it would be a wise investment for the orchestra leadership to provide proper equipment to protect from hearing loss. Everyone has differing degrees of tolerance, but noise-exposure measurements throughout a week of rehearsals and performances can determine if decibel levels present an occupational hazard, and specialists can recommend equipment to alleviate the potential danger.

Conductors do not typically encounter the problem unless the soloists are using electronics to amplify the sound. The brass and percussion are located at some distance from the podium, and the strings cannot play loudly enough to cause harm. Only the piccolo has high notes that can be difficult on the ear. The damage we more commonly suffer is pain in the lower back, shoulders, and neck. Sometimes the strain on the arms can lead to some muscular problems, but overall, we do stay in relatively decent shape.

I could add stabbing oneself with a baton, falling off the podium, and cutting a finger during a page turn to the list of perils. All these have happened to me. Once in a while, in the case of a few conductors, the injuries have been serious. I saw Bernstein topple off the rostrum while trying to shake hands with the first desk players in the Vienna Philharmonic. He fell onto his chest while wearing a medallion honoring Dimitri Mitropoulos.

Pianists have endured bleeding fingers from glissandi. Cellists have had a string snap and strike them in the face. Wind players run the risk of instruments getting pushed accidently into their mouths and possibly losing some teeth. There is not enough space to write about the potential hazards with percussion instruments.

All we know is that these problems are not going away. Some are inevitable, and most are accidental. Others come from unseen dangers, such as coronavirus. We cannot prepare for every eventuality. At best, we can exercise caution, but at the same time, we cannot compromise our artistic integrity. No one outside the industry sees music as a high-risk profession. But such are the times we live in. We are required to behave like others as we travel, attend public events, and go about our daily lives, but we always need to remember that because we are musicians, we are not like others.

19

ON AUDITIONS

Extroverts may get places faster, but for introverts it's all about working at the pace you need and, at the end of the day, performing at your best.

—Douglas Conant

"Not again! Slatkin, you have already written at least twice in this book about the audition process. We know what you think about changing the rules as well as one possible solution to being more inclusive when it comes to diversity in our orchestras. Why are you writing again on the subject?"

Good question, and one which will be answered henceforth.

Over the course of my entire career, I have received many requests from musicians, agents, and parents who want me to hear their prodigies, artists, and offspring. These advocates do not contact me with the hope that I might help their protégés get a job in an orchestra but rather with the idea that I might engage them as soloists. I have certainly heard several thousand auditions over the last half-century.

You know the appellation "stage" mother. I am here to tell you that it applies equally to dads. When I began my professional work as assistant conductor in St. Louis, letters and phone calls started to pour in, and I tried to listen to as many auditions as possible, whether for possible inclusion in the orchestra's various series or for membership in the newly created ensemble for kids.

Six weeks before the very first rehearsal of the St. Louis Symphony Youth Orchestra in 1970, I spent my Saturdays listening to violinists, pianists, clarinetists—and there were a lot of them—as well as any other child instrumentalist who signed up. There was even an accordionist and a harmonica player.

Although there were some talents in the group, no one really stood out enough to make me want to engage them as a soloist, even for a children's concert. Once the youth orchestra was up and running, we were able to cultivate higher-level performance standards. Eventually we decided to have a competition for young artists. If the candidates were good, one or two might play with the junior symphony, and if they were really great, they might appear with the parent organization, albeit not on subscription programs.

Observing the demeanor of those auditioning for the solo slot was instructive. Some played from memory, but most chose not to. In almost every case, their body language conveyed that playing was more of a duty than a pleasure. This was apparently a common manifestation of nerves among younger musicians. A few of them had a more extreme response to the audition experience that consisted of walking onstage, looking out into the almost 3,000-seat auditorium, and abruptly leaving without playing a note. Parents were not allowed into the hall.

My job was fairly straightforward. I asked their name and what they were going to play. When they finished, or in some instances when I stopped them, I just said, "Thank you," and that was it. There was no feedback, even though I kept notes and considered sending remarks to the aspiring musicians. But if I had done that, it likely would have started an unending string of letters. To the more than 600 applicants who auditioned for the youth orchestra in the first year, we either sent a "thumbs up" or a polite "no." Everyone was encouraged to try again the following year.

How do young people ready themselves for such an experience? A music instructor can help by ensuring that the students are well prepared and encouraging them to try their best. If they do not get chosen, the teacher should simply assure them that they will do better next time while continuing to help them develop their tone and musicality before the next audition. Parents have to be particularly careful not to interfere with what the teacher is doing. The young musician cannot have conflicting ideas on how to approach playing for others.

I listened to a number of other auditions in those early years. In particular, members of the board of directors had their own prodigies they wanted to promote. This was an extremely tricky path to navigate, as the decision of whether or not to book a soloist who was endorsed by a governing member of the organization carried potential financial implications. Thankfully, Music Director Walter Susskind called the shots. Overall, these were more seasoned musicians but hardly at the level of the vast majority of artists who appeared with the orchestra. If they were deemed good enough, these performers were usually passed off to me, rarely getting to the subscription concert stage. I was young enough that any experience was worth it. Working with soloists that exhibited memory lapses, fistfuls of wrong notes, and almost unbearable stage fright, I learned a great deal about how to handle the issues many artists confronted, lessons that would help me throughout my career.

On one occasion, in Washington, DC, we were performing a work that required a boy soprano. Whenever this voice is needed for a work, it is critical to have a second one standing by, just in case there might be the overnight change of register. After the first of three concerts, the young boy suddenly became a man, and we had to make the appropriate substitution. His parents were furious. What I had not known previously was that this child was the son of the secretary of energy; I fully expected the power supply at my house to be cut off immediately.

Sometimes I received requests from distinguished teachers who wanted me to listen to their charges. If I knew the instructor, he or she would assure me that it would be worth my time, and this proved true. Whether suggesting potential soloists for the annual *Messiah* performances or just introducing me to a pianist to keep an eye on, these teachers were an invaluable resource for discovering new artists. I certainly remember the time when I was asked to listen to an eleven-year-old cellist who might have some possibilities. Yo-Yo Ma, as well as other talents such as Midori, Josh Bell, and so many others, made their orchestral or tour debuts with me as a direct result of teacher recommendations and an in-person audition.

With annual trips to New York in my concert calendar, I always made a point of taking a full day to listen to mostly young musicians. I would secure a room at The Juilliard School, and my regular assistant, Suzanne Leek, would come along to make sure everything ran on time. The performers usually started off with part of a concerto, then a couple of shorter pieces. These were tough days, as I normally had to lead a concert that night.

One difference in the audition process for these young people as opposed to those that auditioned for me at the beginning of my career is that I would take a minute to chat with them. It might have been about the instrument they were playing, their concerto repertoire, or even where they might see themselves in ten years. Interaction, in my experience, can make all the difference if the person auditioning shows some signs of nervousness. That is one reason I favor taking the screen down for the semifinal round of orchestra auditions. Oh, I forgot that I wasn't going to write about this anymore.

These annual and sometimes twice-a-year auditions eventually included some agents. By that time, I had become acquainted with many of the artist managers personally and did not feel uncomfortable with them attending, but I always asked the musician if it was okay for them to stay and listen. The same invitation to observe was extended to the teachers, but usually they opted out. Sometimes artistic administrators from my orchestra and others would pop in as well. In these situations, the more people who hear the audition, the better the soloist's odds of getting an engagement, assuming that the talent is there.

Singers also auditioned for me. In these cases, I asked in advance that they perform works from different styles and in at least three different languages. The clever ones knew that I did not do that much work in opera and would usually sing just one aria alongside selections from cantatas, song cycles, or even Broadway shows. Looking back over my program archives, I was amazed to discover how many of them I hired over all these years.

Sometimes musicians just want to play for me to seek advice rather than an engagement. When I have time, I am more than happy to oblige. Maybe I can pass along a recommendation to others. Conductors seeking the attention of music directors and artistic administrators have the benefit of today's technology, which allows us to see them in action. While we cannot judge the true interaction with the members of the orchestra, we can assess most of the technical skills via video. Composers simply need to send us their scores and, if possible, a recording of a performance.

My father once told me that he never got nervous. "Why should I? After practicing, studying, feeling that I know the music, and trying my best, that is all I can do. And if I have not done those things, not only should I be nervous, I shouldn't be out there playing in the first place."

That pretty much sums it up. Solid preparation is the key to success at an audition.

My advice is as follows: Try to display confidence, even if some passages are not coming out the way you wished. Auditions rarely go perfectly. Wear appropriate attire when you are playing for anyone. As much as we would like to believe that looks don't matter in music, they do. Be comfortable but not sloppy.

Play a few notes before you begin your first piece. Get a feeling for the space and acoustics. If something goes awry at the start, just ask if you can begin again. No one will hold this against you. Once you start, go into your own world of sound. It does no good to second guess yourself or to focus on what the listeners are thinking. Stay with your own vision for the music. Be yourself so that the individuality you possess comes through.

And of course, the same rules apply if you are auditioning for an orchestra position. Dammit! I did it again.

20

ON EDUCATION

Every student has something to offer, and every student
deserves a nurturing learning environment.

—Ilhan Omar

Most of us who have achieved any degree of success in the arts
can identify several teachers or mentors whose wisdom and
experience helped mold our artistry. Although we may have rebelled
against their influence for a time, in looking back, we realize the
importance of these special advisors.

Of utmost significance are those who nurture us when we are
very young. As a child, I was surrounded by some of the most talented composers and performers in the world, but my fourth-grade
music teacher, Mrs. Otto, made an equally valuable contribution
to my early music education. She came to our class twice a week
and introduced our young minds and hearts to the world of abstract
sound. Strumming away on the Autoharp, she fired up our imagina-
tions by encouraging us to join in with whatever sounds we wanted
to add to the mix.

I had other influential educators, as during my youth, music
programs in the public-school system in Los Angeles were abundant.
Classes in the arts did not take place before or after regular school
hours but were part of the curriculum. They were required, whether
band, chorus, orchestra, painting, pottery, or any of the other creative activities that shaped our minds.

But that was back in the 1950s and early 1960s. My, how things have changed. We no longer sit around the radio with our family, listening together. Our religious institutions mostly provide music as a background, once in a while dipping into communal sing, which often seems more like a ritual rather than a joyous experience. And our schools gave up a long time ago.

I received a note from conductor Tim Franklin in which he sheds light on the state of public-school music programs these days:

> In many ways, music education in American public schools has shifted away from nurturing a love for music through discovery and performance and moved into the arena of competitive events and used as an agent for public relations and athletic background music. Frank Battisti, former conductor of the New England Conservatory Wind Ensemble, stated: "Band program experiences often consist of too much activity and not enough art." This problem does not solely lie in the area of the band experience but exists in all areas of music education. There are many fine music educators and offerings throughout the country, but cutbacks have resulted in fewer school districts in the United States having a guiding voice and advocate for true music education. Each year more school music offerings are removed. Even now a school board in Massachusetts has voted to remove all music programs for the 2020–2021 academic year. Some of the greatest music, art, and literature in American history was created during the Depression. It was a connecting point, places of beauty and hope amid the financial downturn and the storms of World War II brewing in Europe and the Pacific Rim. Will music survive in American schools?[1]

When I arrived in Washington, DC, one of the first things I did was attend a meeting of the Board of Education in Fairfax County. They were listening to arguments from the public regarding which elements of the school system's budget should be cut. There was a proposal to eliminate the fourth-grade string orchestra as well as fine- and performing-arts field trips to the District for the students. I spoke rather passionately about my own experience when I was a young person and reminded many of the council members that they probably had the same opportunity to participate in music during elementary school.

They decided not to eliminate the program, but the issue came up again in subsequent years when the school district faced a funding shortfall. Arts advocates have had to continually fight to keep the music alive. It is easy to blame budgetary constraints for the lack of meaningful arts education. Moreover, in today's world of visual media, it is increasingly difficult to find meaning in something intangible, like music. But I do have a proposal regarding the return of an arts agenda in the public-school system.

First of all, we must realize that the government is not going to help out. Funding by federal, state, and city organizations is long gone. What a difference from the days when our nation felt compelled to cherish its art during the Great Depression and Second World War. The National Archives offered this summary of the unprecedented ways in which the federal government supported the arts between 1933 and 1943 for its exhibit, "A New Deal for the Arts":

> The New Deal arts projects provided work for jobless artists, but they also had a larger mission: to promote American art and culture and to give more Americans access to what President Franklin Roosevelt described as "an abundant life." The projects saved thousands of artists from poverty and despair and enabled Americans all across the country to see an original painting for the first time, attend their first professional live theater, or take their first music or drawing class.[2]

As of this writing, we are going through the toughest time since that conflagration—maybe even worse, as public displays of art, especially live, in-person performances, are discouraged due to the need to isolate. All of us are feeling Zoom fatigue, and trying to teach the arts via internet leaves out the fundamental need for personalization. There is a potential solution, both for this time and beyond.

I would like you to think about the following: From 1803 to 1804, Ludwig van Beethoven wrote his Third Symphony. It revolutionized music, perhaps more than any other previous piece. But it also reflected a turning point in political history that informed the title of the work that we know today: "Eroica." The composer had the highest admiration for Napoleon. Here was a man who stood for the ideals of democracy and anti-monarchical thinking. The original name for this work was "Bonaparte."

After the symphony was completed, but prior to its first performance, Beethoven's personal secretary, Ferdinand Ries, informed the master that something significant had taken place:

> I was the first to tell him the news that Buonaparte had declared himself Emperor, whereupon he broke into a rage and exclaimed, "So he is no more than a common mortal! Now, too, he will tread under foot all the rights of Man, indulge only his ambition; now he will think himself superior to all men, become a tyrant!" Beethoven went to the table, seized the top of the title-page, tore it in half and threw it on the floor. The page had to be recopied, and it was only now that the symphony received the title "Sinfonia eroica."[3]

Figure 20.1.   First page of the "Eroica" by Ludwig van Beethoven. *Credit:* **Mondadori Portfolio/Contributor, Getty Images**

Figure 20.2. Opening page of the score for Beethoven's Symphony No. 3 ("Eroica")

In addition to renaming the symphony, Beethoven added the sub-title, proclaiming that the piece was "composed to celebrate the memory of a great man." It was as if Beethoven was scorning his former hero. The work went on to have a lasting impact on the musical world.

There are conflicting reports as to what the composer actually did to the first page. He might have thrown the whole score on the floor or even ripped up pages. Upon examination of the manuscript, we can see that the composer scratched out the initial dedication (see figure 20.1).

That sets us up for the stunning first two bars of the piece, described by Leonard Bernstein as "thunderbolts from Zeus" and "hammer blows from Thor" (see figure 20.2).

Keep in mind that Beethoven had completed the symphony prior to the declaration from Napoleon, so those first two bars already existed. But conductors and musicians have had lengthy discussions as to what they represent. Some believe that these first chords should convey a sense of dignity and nobility in keeping with the symphonist's depiction of his hero. Others think that they should be played aggressively, reflecting the anger Beethoven felt for the betrayal. On YouTube you can hear many of the different ways these opening notes are performed.[4]

Using these examples, teachers can easily trace the artistic culture of the time to give students a visual and aural window into the Napoleonic era. Through this approach, studying history is no longer just about reading but becomes a more immersive experience. Other art forms can be incorporated into the curriculum as well, such as architecture, sculpture, and painting. The days of yore come to life in an entirely different way when multiple senses are engaged.

All art is connected to the time in which it is created. Perhaps it is regarded as forward-looking or retrogressive, but each creation is a product of its own era. Even if the work is simply Symphony No. 3, without an extramusical connotation, there is still a relationship with what was occurring in the outside world at the time of its writing, whether or not the artist intended it. This is certainly also true of popular culture, and we should therefore not focus solely on what is generally thought of as "the classics." If we are to connect with the young people of today, we have to understand how they feel, what they react to, and why they seemingly reject so much of the past.

So how do we accomplish such an ambitious undertaking in public education? What I propose is a philanthropic foundation created for the express purpose of developing an arts curriculum that would be passed on to history teachers in the public-school system. I would suggest that the curriculum include at least six art forms: music, painting, architecture, sculpture, dance, and poetry.

During the months of June, July, and August, the foundation would sponsor three four-week symposiums devoted to training teachers. Six days a week, faculty would teach classes in each of the arts subjects. These instructors would be selected on the basis of their educational skills as well as their passion for their area of interest by a panel consisting of foundation members with a background in education and the arts.

The history teachers would apply to be participants. Their CVs would be reviewed by the faculty, and twenty-five educators would be selected for each symposium. Over the course of four weeks, a total of twenty-four lessons would be given in each of the six subjects, with the final class being a wrap-up session devoted to implementing what was learned. A manual for teaching would be presented to each of the educators, providing guidelines for adapting the material to the classroom environment. Integrating the arts into the history curriculum would commence at the beginning of the school year, when the seventy-five teachers would share the results of their training with several thousand students. This initial phase of the project would last for three years, and if proven successful, satellite programs could be established in different parts of the country.

That is a very rough idea of how the institute would work. The big question has to do with how to pay for it. Again, I would caution that the government is not going to assist, and as I am writing this, we are at the beginning of one of the worst fiscal crises in history. But there are those with vision who see why the arts are a vital part of society. Over the years, I have noticed that when the purse strings are tight, philanthropists and even members of the general public are more than thrilled to help out when it comes to education.

Many orchestras create programs that bring aspiring musicians together. In Detroit, on any given Saturday, more than five hundred young people gather at Orchestra Hall to participate in the Wu Family Academy for Learning and Engagement. They play in orchestras, participate in master classes, and are given instruments if they do not have one. Endowment gifts come much easier when you explain that the money will be used for education and outreach. The days of donors just writing a blank check to the organization are over.

More than likely, we are looking at a two-million-dollar start-up fee to cover the salaries for the faculty, a stipend for the teachers, housing, and expenses related to developing the education materials. Many costs can be minimized with the use of current technology.

There are several possibilities for where the foundation activities would take place. My own thoughts lean toward a university, with perhaps a tie-in with that school's arts departments. It is also possible to conduct the symposium as an online webinar. This is not quite as effective as an intense personal experience through which the attendees and faculty could interact more directly, but it certainly could keep costs down. However, since the goal is to really get the teachers to engage their students in the classroom environment, it would be preferable for all of them to come to one place.

Learning about the arts does not mean, by any stretch of the imagination, that everyone will be rushing out to be a musician, sculptor, or dancer. Nevertheless, integrating the arts into the classroom deepens capacities for creative problem-solving, attentiveness, memory, communication, and collaboration that students can use across all disciplines. Ultimately, such an education satisfies our hearts, minds, and souls.

We are facing a critical time for the arts, and it is vital that we find a way to place culture on equal footing with the other building blocks of a fine education. Incorporating the arts into the existing curriculum is a logical and affordable way to encourage meaningful discovery.

21

THE ROAD TO RECOVERY

Headlines, in a way, are what mislead you because bad news is a headline, and gradual improvement is not.

—Bill Gates

The vast majority of this book was written during the year of our discontent. As musicians, we could not present our art to an in-person public and were forced, as were so many others, into devising new ways to keep ourselves occupied.

Conductors were among the hardest hit, as they no longer had their instrument—an ensemble—to practice with. It was already a lonely enough profession. Some of us felt a stronger bond with composers as we spent more time absorbing what they had to teach us through their scores.

Reflecting on the scope of the pandemic, I counted myself lucky. I have led a great life so far, with many opportunities to grow and maintain a career in my chosen profession over the past half-century. Speaking to younger conductors on various platforms during this period of uncertainty, I could sense their anxiety about the future of the orchestra business and their own financial well-being. Who could accurately predict when, if ever, we would even assume a degree of normality amid rising infection and death rates, staggering unemployment figures, and market volatility? Large swaths of society refused to listen to the scientists and doctors. As racial tensions mounted, the 1960s were returning with a vengeance, and the political divide in the country made some dialogue completely impossible.

Over the course of several months, I tried to understand and explain to those who read my blog what I believed was going on. More importantly, I tried to offer some suggestions regarding how we might return to music-making.

In rereading those posts, it seemed like a good idea to share a selection of these pieces, each of which captures a particular moment during the pandemic. In retrospect, I have found that many of my early predictions came true. By the time this book is published, hopefully our progress as an industry and a society will render some of my solutions moot. However, I hope you find these essays interesting to read as food for thought while we continue to navigate our way through unprecedented times.

Here is to all of you. Stay healthy and stay safe.

MAY 29, 2020

There is nothing like returning to a place that remains unchanged to find the ways in which you yourself have altered.

—Nelson Mandela

Nearly three months into the process of isolating ourselves physically from the rest of society, members of the arts world find themselves struggling to come up with solutions for how to return, if we really do, to a more regular pattern of life. This has given us a lot to think about, and this pondering has produced some interesting experiments.

Performances are given with musicians all over the world participating, their images projected onto our devices as if they were an extended version of the *Brady Bunch*. I was involved in one webinar with eight other people and found myself in the middle of the three-across group. All of a sudden, I was Paul Lynde on *Hollywood Squares*.

There is no question that the entertainment world, along with sports and other large-venue events, will not be functioning normally for a long time. Those who think that come the fall everything related to COVID-19 will simply disappear are in for an unfortunate surprise.

Rather than dwelling on what has been, I would like to use this space to project what I believe might be practical to achieve with limitations on in-person gatherings. Realizing that organizations are planning to start up again, albeit with precautions in place, I have been thinking about what can be done in terms of programming and logistics. Let's begin with the musicians.

We have seen experiments with smaller orchestral ensembles practicing social distancing. Depending on the size of the stage, it may be possible to have up to forty-or-so musicians, plus a conductor, on the platform at the same time. That will more than likely be the way of the world for a while. But it is that separation that makes things so unlike what we have ever practiced. Even though some don't like it, the closer an instrumentalist is to another one, the better the balance and ensemble, as well as the intonation. Additionally, there are some other major impediments to staying apart.

Almost every time I have conducted a Haydn symphony, for example, when we get to the repeat in the first movement, there is inevitably a page turn immediately followed by a continuation of the violin part and sometimes all the other instruments. That is why we have two people on a stand in the string section, a practice that has been in place for a couple of centuries. One has to stop playing and then quickly and adroitly negotiate turning the page so all will go smoothly.

But without stand partners to perform this action, the music will simply have to stop. There is no way around that, is there? Well, maybe there is. Some musicians are beginning to use tablets and can accomplish page turns by tapping a foot pedal. It is not impossible to envision this as a wave of the future for orchestras. It would require an initial investment on the part of the organization to purchase tablets, stylus pens, and software, but one that might be offset over time by savings in printing costs and labor.

Uploading materials and distributing them to the musicians would be the responsibility of the librarians. After putting markings into a master set, rather than having to transfer those markings into each printed part, they would send the relevant master file to each member of the orchestra. Any alterations by others involved in future performances could be added to the existing electronic master set. The other plus is that no one has to physically touch the device other than the player. After all, we certainly cannot perform with gloves on.

With the ensemble spread out, how can its members properly hear each other? There is an assumption that this job of balancing is sorted out by the conductor. But in order to accomplish this, the musicians have to be in close proximity to one another, so they can hear what their colleagues are up to. It is just not possible to coordinate everything with the musicians so far apart. The issue of immediate communication is lost with distancing.

The solution is one that has been in play with pop artists for years. Audio monitors are strategically placed onstage, allowing the performers to hear what the other musicians are playing. You have all seen this setup numerous times but may have assumed that it is for overall volume level. No, it is to help with coordinating the musicians when they cannot hear each other onstage as clearly as they would like. Assuming that it can be done discreetly, why not try it out with an orchestra? Again, this has been done before with pops concerts, and a few composers require it for certain pieces.

It is not necessary to employ click tracks, used primarily for film and television in order to synchronize the music and picture. They are impractical for the majority of concert works because they preclude flexibility. You have to stay with the ticking metronome that is heard by the musicians via a small headphone or earbud. During a concert, there always has to be room for change and spontaneity.

We have now partially solved two problems. Let's add a small chorus to the mix.

When you see those vocalists onstage, they always look like sardines, packed in tightly. Everyone has their own score, so they always know what the other musicians are playing or singing. Each accomplishes the page turns with little or no effort. And they can hear each other very well, depending on the setup the chorus master chooses to employ. Robert Shaw positioned his forces in quartets rather than just putting the sopranos on the left and basses on the right. Clearly that would not be practical given distancing requirements. More than likely we would have to put a couple of monitors in for them as well as the orchestra.

The last work I conducted was a rehearsal of Orff's *Carmina Burana* in Detroit. This was on the very day that the National Basketball Association suspended its season and the governor of Michigan urged organizations to cancel or postpone large gatherings after the state's first two cases of coronavirus were confirmed. We practiced with the chorus out in the audience seats, but the orchestra was still packed in onstage. With the ability to stream all our concerts in Detroit, there was the thought of performing *Carmina* this way and broadcasting it to the world without the public in attendance.

That did not work out, but I thought of one problem that might occur no matter how we did it. What if any one person coughed or sneezed? We have statistics that tell us how far air molecules travel under different circumstances. It is clear that everyone would need to be more than six feet apart to mitigate that risk. And it goes without saying that having vocalists wear masks is just not going to work. The same, even more obviously, is true for the woodwind and brass players in the orchestra.

Nope. Chorus performances are on hold indefinitely. Let's move on to the audience.

This is complicated, but not in the way you might think. We have models that tell us how to get them into the auditorium. My own thought is that first, we need temperature scanners for each person coming in. Patrons from the same household sit next to each other, but three empty seats separate them from other parties. This looks strange, but all of us have played to what looks like near-empty houses. We try to give our all no matter the size of the crowd.

Remember how I wrote about smaller ensembles being the rule for a while? Here is my solution, as regards programming—not elegant but practical.

First of all, it is becoming clear that most full-size orchestras will not be able to go forward with the season's programming as it has been announced and still observe social distancing guidelines. No more Mahler Six, Copland Three, or *Carmina Burana*. There needs to be an alternative program in place now, so we can be ready to respond to government restrictions and adapt to the recommendations of the health authorities. I am quite surprised, with just a little over three months before the start of the new season, that no orchestra has asked me to have an alternate program ready in case the originally planned one cannot be performed due to orchestra size.

When it comes to soloists, as well as conductors, a new problem emerges. If there is a resurgence of the virus and either or both decide not to travel, what options are possible? Here is an interesting thought. Each orchestra could engage a conductor from within the community, or a member of the orchestra, to lead the programs. There are always one or two who can do a good job. The day of assistantships in the United States has slowly been evaporating in favor of freelance "cover" conductors hired by the week. Having someone on the staff helps ensure that there is always a person available to lead the concerts.

Does it require a new mindset? Absolutely. But we are all anxious to get back to doing what we are driven to do. Even if only a couple hundred people are in the hall, our job is to make music at the highest possible level. With creative solutions, we can ease ourselves into the new world. And after that, who knows what we will all want? Maybe changes like this can provide more flexibility; we might even hold on to a few of the models.

And on the off chance that come the fall, the virus miraculously vanishes, a vaccine is developed in time for the next wave, and society is functioning in the way it used to, we can put this idea on the back burner, just in case. There are so many possibilities, and I wanted to get these first thoughts out now. But in a couple of weeks there will be a follow-up, with other ideas for a new way forward. Keep watching this space.

JUNE 7, 2020

> Art is for healing ourselves, and everybody needs their own personal art to heal up their problems.
>
> —Linda Ronstadt

A little over a week ago, I wrote at length about what concert life might look like as we get to September and October, the start of the cultural season. I considered matters of orchestra size, social distancing among musicians and audience members, how to accommodate subscribers, and other pressing matters.

In the short time between that article and this one, I have heard from a number of people in the profession, many of whom are trying to formulate similar thoughts and put a plan in place. My piece left out some factors that must be considered, each of them affecting the process of returning to the concert hall. Perhaps it might be easiest for me to address some of these issues by framing them in the form of questions:

1. *You wrote about the necessity of social distancing in the hall. Since that will mean a greatly reduced number of patrons, how can we decide who gets first preference for tickets?*

   This is clearly a delicate subject. Prior to the shutdown, most orchestras were starting to find their way in attracting new and younger audiences. But the subscriber base still remains the backbone of the audience, determining how our musical institutions predict box office revenue as well as indicating who attends concerts.

   I would have to say that those are the people who come first. In the course of a regular season, the subscribers are those who get the initial messages about what is going to be performed in the next year—they have the opportunity to renew, keep their same seats or change, and even create their own series packages. They are owed the chance to pick and choose among the revised offerings before anyone else. I would also include those who are new subscribers as well.

   If you read the previous post, you know that I proposed smaller-sized ensembles onstage as well as reduced capacity in the hall. But in order to do that and still accommodate the number of people who might come to hear a concert, the number of repeat performances would have to increase. Under this new plan, subscribers would have options for different concert days and times than previously offered. There might be up to eight choices of the same program in a given week. In some cases, decisions will have to be made when one performance reaches the maximum capacity allowed for distancing purposes.

This is when all those years of building the subscriber base and creating personal interactions with the audience come into play. The audience comprises not only those who attend concerts but also those persons whose contributions extend far beyond sitting and enjoying. It is their fiscal support, as individuals and corporations, that keeps an orchestra afloat, and strengthening connections with this constituency needs to remain a priority.

One of the reasons I began to write about this potential new concert experience was because when orchestras do start up again, it cannot be with just a few days' notice. With the new season three months or so away, information has to go out to the public soon. I estimate that contingencies would need to be in place at least two months before the first scheduled event to sort out issues related to reduced audience capacity in a way that demonstrates gratitude to donors, rewards subscriber loyalty, and includes room for attracting new audiences. This will require a thoughtful approach and an incredibly creative marketing strategy.

2. *Okay, suppose you can accommodate four hundred people for each performance. It still looks like a pretty empty house to the musicians. Won't they be just a bit depressed seeing this paucity of audience members week after week?*

Not at all. We know that we are playing for the people who are there, irrespective of how many. Given what we have been going through, my suspicion is that everyone will be glad to be making music together, even if they are apart. All of us have performed for, shall we say, intimate-sized audiences. We appreciate that they have come to the concert, and sometimes, our best performances have been heard by only a few.

3. *Won't you run out of repertoire if this model continues too long?*

Think about it a different way. When have you last heard your orchestra play a series of Haydn symphonies, portions of the Romantic repertoire with smaller forces, or even

Bach? I would look upon this as an adventure, exploring pieces not usually heard but still important in the repertoire. Mozart, Schubert, and even Beethoven can take on a fresh, new meaning in this context.

In the 20th and this first part of the 21st century, a lot of music has been written for chamber orchestra. Stravinsky, Bartók, Hindemith, and Copland all have a number of works that would be nice to encounter again. This is also a time for creative commissioning, should we have a second wave of the virus.

It is also a time to relax some of the restrictions that have made performing some masterpieces cost-prohibitive under current agreements. Most orchestras have a set number of musicians who must be onstage in order to avoid incurring extra payments to the players. I would have loved to do the Gran Partita by Mozart for thirteen instruments, or the Stravinsky Octet, for example, but there are financial considerations associated with programming them.

4. *There will still be musicians and audience members who are not comfortable returning to the concert hall, even after restrictions are relaxed. How can we keep them involved?*

Once again, we are confronted with rules that have governed how we export our musical product. So many orchestras could not broadcast performances from their archives due to the expense of having to pay the musicians for work they might have done a long time ago. It is my feeling that for the time being, we should open up the extensive libraries so the listening public can hear presentations from years gone by. The treasure trove of works, artists, and composers is incredible.

I have conducted numerous premieres, many of which were only heard by people who attended the concerts. At the very least, we should all be allowed to hear music that has only been listened to by a limited number of audience members. If we are to preserve art and possibly discover something worthy of future consideration, these performances need to be made available. And until we return to some kind of normal, if we ever do, these presentations should be made free to the public, without financial compensation to the performers. This is an investment in bringing audiences back.

In Detroit, the DSO has opened up its on-demand video streaming archive for free online access, providing a new avenue through which to share the power of music with a wider audience. Several of the DSO players have hosted "Watch Parties" during broadcasts of archival concerts on social media, taking time to speak with fans about the music, their lives, and what they have been doing during this quarantine period. Other ensembles have also become creative with offerings that audiences can enjoy from home. The public now can put faces to names and instruments, hopefully making for a more personal relationship when concert life resumes.

Many orchestras have a rich archive that needs to be mined. Most of it is audio, but even early videos are surfacing. Preserving that history is only valuable if we can access it. Music is not meant to sit in some library, unseen or unheard.

5. *How has this lockdown affected music education, and what can we do to move forward?*

Here is perhaps the most important question of all. Although orchestras have placed the teaching of music to young people as a priority, they are limited in the number of students they reach. This is a visual age, but even with the use of technology, there is still nothing like the personal relationship of a music teacher working face-to-face with individuals or groups.

Almost every teacher of an instrument, or voice, will tell you that they have struggled to figure out how to instruct without hearing the true sound being produced. One can show how a passage is fingered, the hand position, or whether something is up or down bow. Ultimately, though, the resonance is being relayed via a microphone and speaker. No matter how sophisticated, it does not compare to the real thing. For the teacher, this has to be the most frustrating aspect of social distancing.

For composers, perhaps it is a little bit easier. One can project the scores and parts onto a screen and have a discussion about what is presented. Even orchestration can be taught this way. With the various music composition software available, at least a representation of how a piece might sound is possible.

As for general music education, this is a good time to be creative. Finding ways to represent music via a visual experience is certainly a consideration. Normally I am against this kind of thing in the concert hall. Most music is abstract and requires the imagination to generate images in the mind. Perhaps teaching young people to create visuals to go along with what they are hearing is a possibility. A class project might involve the entire group creating a piece of music together. For older students, I would suggest looking up the Music in the Air (MITA) program, which has the most extensive music teaching library I know of.[1]

6. *With auditions postponed, how will orchestras fill vacancies in their rosters?*

Hmm. There is no question that these cannot be held any way other than in person, at least from the semifinals onward. Wind or brass players would usually be asked to play in a small ensemble with other members of the section involved. In an upcoming book, I give an example of a new model for auditions. Still, it is pretty clear that orchestras will not be able to go forward with auditioning new musicians for the time being.

As mentioned in my last web piece, we will all have to get along with smaller ensembles for a while. One of the reasons is that there will be a delay in the process of selecting new members to join the orchestra. Another is that there will be musicians in the orchestra who are reluctant to return until they feel physically and mentally prepared to come back. Relying on the freelance pool in our communities is really the only solution.

Since I am no longer a music director, I am not up-to-date on the exact number of vacancies or postponed auditions, but certainly this crisis has disrupted the process for all orchestras, and I suppose auditions will continue to be canceled for the next few months. This is another reason for getting alternate programs, utilizing reduced forces, in place right now, so that the musicians and public know what the alternatives will be.

Basically, the answer to the question is that we cannot go forward with auditions at this time. Some will argue that the screened auditions make the social distancing easy. But think of how many candidates will be reluctant to travel, thereby reducing the potential pool of musicians taking an audition and hampering the orchestra's goal to attract as many qualified candidates as possible.

7. *What happens to fundraising and how will the orchestra and staff be paid?*

Every cultural institution has its own method of dealing with this issue, as does virtually any business. With no income from ticket sales, almost all revenue will be coming in the form of donations. A few groups will be borrowing from the principal of their endowments, but that is not ideal.

Most orchestral institutions worked out pay reductions for the musicians and members of the staff. It is doubtful that even this lower level of compensation can be sustained should the virus resurface, or even if it holds steady. Only a large downturn in risk of resurgence or the development of a vaccine will get us back to the conditions we were used to. It will still take a long time to recover from the fiscal impact of lost income.

Ultimately, arts organizations are at the mercy and generosity of their patrons. It is possible that many will be inspired by the creative ways the orchestras are finding to bring music to the public during this time of separation. There is no way to know what kind of financial shape we will be in as the new year approaches.

8. *In your previous post, you wrote about alternate programs that might replace the originally scheduled ones. But if we have an intermission, aren't we talking about a potential risk that might be avoided?*

Good point. Another manner of presentation certainly could be concerts without a break. We have seen these even when the full orchestra was present. The idea of shorter programs with strong content has always been viable. The hour of the event could be early evening so that people can attend after work but before dinner.

Taking this and including the model of two separate groups of forty-or-so musicians, it is even possible to conceive of a day on which four performances might take place, especially over the weekend. Each orchestra would play the same program. The first one does theirs at 11:00 a.m. and 1:30 p.m. Orchestra B starts at 7:00 p.m. and then plays again at 9:30 p.m. If each program lasts a maximum of an hour and fifteen minutes, we don't even have a predicament with overtime.

The people who would suffer from this arrangement would be the concessionaires, who rely on food and drink sales. Perhaps some combination of full-length concerts and abbreviated performances without intermission over the course of one week is the most workable of the alternatives. Each organization would have to sort that out in terms of what can be accomplished with the staff and musicians, and what the audiences will accept.

There will certainly be more questions, and it is possible that the first few months of resumed artistic activities will be confusing. No one ever said that art is easy, but it is vital at times like these, with social unrest creating tension in addition to the ongoing pandemic. Our economy is in shambles, making it even more difficult to project what it will be like as we attempt to move forward.

However, that is what is required of all of us who create and re-create. If we can touch even a few souls again, we will be reminded of one of the principal reasons we became part of the music world—to share meaningful and inspirational experiences with others.

JUNE 14, 2020

Human history becomes more and more a race between
education and catastrophe.

—H. G. Wells

Perspective has a way of reshaping our priorities. For the past two
weeks, we have witnessed events that either remind us of earlier
times or, for the younger set, are unlike anything we have ever experienced. Now we can truly say "The Whole World Is Watching."

I remember 1968 very well. Although my heart and soul went
into my studies, it was impossible to be immune to the scenes in
Grant Park—and in major cities and college towns across the country—as Americans were reeling from the assassinations of Martin
Luther King Jr. and Robert Kennedy as well as the continuing
conflict in Vietnam. Here we find ourselves once again, grappling
with social and political unrest and physical acts of violence that are
changing on a daily basis. This time, however, our war is not against
an enemy in a faraway country, and we know why we are fighting.

Seeing people flagrantly gathering together, sans masks and
without social distancing, was disturbing enough. But the horrendous sight of military force being used against our own civilians was
not just a reminder of fifty-two years ago but also reminiscent of
demonstrations in so many other countries whose governments have
made no pretext about the reasons for such crackdowns. No wonder
the plight of our musical community seems almost insignificant at
times like these.

But as we begin to emerge from the cocoon, not at all sure if
we will have to return to our enclosures at some point, it is not too
soon to consider our futures as well as the wild cards that will most
certainly be in the deck.

My own conducting schedule does not resume until October,
and my first dates are back in Detroit. I have already offered an
alternate program that could work should the orchestra consider a
scenario with reduced forces onstage during the recovery phase. On
the assumption that the industry will not be at 100 percent in terms
of orchestra, audience, and staff when the new season starts, organi-

zations across the country are engaged in contingency planning and establishing the parameters for operations based on potential public health conditions.

For me as a guest artist, travel considerations would be of primary concern. It is about a nine-hour drive to Detroit from St. Louis, which can be done in one day, should I feel unsafe flying. The DSO has an apartment right across the street from the hall. And there is a Whole Foods just a couple hundred feet away. So far, so good.

In my proposed adjustments to the original program, I allowed for the possible change of soloist, should he decide it is not yet the time to travel. It is doubtful that we will have the full orchestra on the stage, and if there is an audience, the hall will be filled to, at most, one quarter of capacity, probably less. Maybe the most practical solution for this dilemma is to do rehearsals as usual and rather than give live concerts, record them with no audience present and later broadcast them through the orchestra's streaming service. That way, the webcast team could edit three "performances" and include additional content such as interviews and commentary on the repertoire while taking the opportunity to try out different camera angles.

But if there is a strong feeling that there should be audience members in attendance, why not make the rehearsals open in this way? Give all subscribers a chance to be part of the experience. Perhaps the concerts themselves, should there be a public presence, should not have an intermission, as it would be impossible to keep social distancing rules in place for gatherings in the foyer. The use of restrooms presents another set of problems.

Do not forget that the scientists and medical professionals are warning that a second wave of the virus is highly likely in the fall, so there will be trepidation among many. If orchestras are to return at all, there must be assurances for all constituents that the environment will be safe. But the above decisions are ones that must be made by every arts organization after careful consideration of the costs and benefits of each scenario. My role is simply to suggest alternatives as regards the music itself, at least outside of these pages.

The next date on my calendar is in Spokane, Washington. Those of you who read these posts on a regular basis know that I have been visiting orchestras in cities where I have never performed, and usually at the request of a good friend. I love doing these, as there are so many wonderful ensembles, not only throughout the States but also all around the world. In just this past week, I have received word that this orchestra is still weighing options for how they are going to handle the fall season.

Again, I have proposed alternate programs for these concerts, but it is possible, as it is for all live events, that they might not occur at all. A lot of us are quite worried about airports, as well as the flights themselves. Even baggage claim presents challenges. Everything is on a wait-and-see basis, but it is more than helpful to have different scenarios in place. I am not a big fan of surprises when it comes to our orchestral life. There are plenty in the music itself.

After the scheduled engagement in Washington State, I have two weeks of teaching on my calendar, one in New York and one in Cleveland. Who knows what the state of affairs will be like at our educational institutions? We will probably not know much until the schools get up and running, if they do at all. Even though clever folks have done wonders with virtual learning, teaching ultimately is about personal connection. There is no way to do anything with an orchestra via Zoom, although I can do a bit of teaching and some webinars if in-person instruction is still on hold.

Then, by the end of October, it is time to go to Europe. It appears that several countries are now starting to present live performances, albeit with fewer people in the audience, and mostly with smaller ensembles. This is where the wild card comes in.

At the moment, most entrants into these countries face a mandatory two-week quarantine. If this is going to continue into the fall, it will not be possible for guest conductors and soloists to do any consecutive dates. And they will have to arrive fourteen days prior to the first rehearsal. This, of course, is not practical. That is one of the reasons my first article on the recovery had to do with making sure that every orchestra has local musicians in place should the scheduled artists not be able to honor the date.

I will be proposing alternate programs, but the isolation issue remains. With five different countries involved in this trip, something may have to be sacrificed along the way. That is a decision I will make in consultation with the orchestras and my management.

Does this all sound too paranoid? No, just realistic in terms of trying to understand what may or may not occur. Maybe all this preparation will not be necessary, and we will all proceed as planned. I seriously doubt it, as we will not have an approved vaccine until at least the new year. The rush to get our economies going could bring renewed outbreaks. Or perhaps it will not make any difference at all. These many lingering questions cause me to look at all possibilities.

We all want to bring the music back, but at the same time, we have to ensure that we do so in a safe environment for everyone concerned.

The expression still holds: "Hope for the best but expect the worst." Maybe the Boy Scouts said it even more succinctly: "Be prepared."

JUNE 17, 2020

> I have hardly anything in common with myself and should stand very quietly in a corner, content that I can breathe.
>
> —Franz Kafka

The sound you have been hearing of late is that of shoes dropping. Three months into the isolation from normalized civilization, a few things are becoming clear.

We are a nation divided in a world that is more insular. Equality seems to be just a word, devoid of meaning for many. The great experiment called democracy is seeing itself torn apart, and we are barely hanging on to our constitutional rights. Our diverse musical culture is trying its best to be relevant, but at the same time, there is no way for artists to do what they do best: communicate in person.

With hopes that we all might be able to come back by the fall, we have begun to understand that we could only expect the unexpected. The big venues realized that having performances in large theaters would be impossible. Perhaps the audiences could be socially distanced, but on the stages of Broadway or the Metropolitan Opera, the artists could not. Logically, and with an eye on the financial impact, these and other organizations have suspended operations until the new year. With any luck, they might be able to commence rehearsals in time for presentations sometime in January.

With clever use of technology, musicians from several orchestras have tried online events during which they could perform remotely and, via click tracks, coordinate with one another rhythmically. Engineers have found ways to make the sound viable and, in several cases, very good. This method has brought back a little of the feeling that we would be okay.

Soloists, including singers, have presented mini-recitals, usually from their homes. This has enabled us to not only hear them again but also learn what they have been reading, as the obligatory backdrop has become their bookshelves. The problem is that tuning in is similar to watching home movies—interesting, but lacking the degree of video or audio quality we have come to expect when the job is handled by the recording professionals.

Europe has been opening up slowly and, in several instances, we have witnessed actual orchestral performances—albeit with reduced forces—a sign that artistic expression is still occurring within our field. Some have felt a twinge of envy and even resentment as photos of highly respected musicians participating in these events have been posted, as if we need reminding of what so many are not allowed to do. The programs themselves have mostly favored a standard-repertoire approach, although if ever there were a time to try something new, this should be it. Nonetheless, the desire to return is so strong that we are grateful for any content.

Having arrived at the middle of June, orchestras in the States are making some very difficult decisions based on scant evidence. No one knows what further havoc the virus could wreak. Even the usually reliable scientists cannot agree on what will happen. With social distancing supposedly in place, many citizens have chosen to forgo masks, not thinking about how dangerous it could be to others. Seeing people outside looks a lot like it did earlier this year.

But it is not the same, is it? We have started seeing the consequences of the big Memorial Day events as well as the protests that erupted throughout the world. "An ounce of prevention" is not really turning into "a pound of cure"—at least not yet. We seem to need no less than a ton of restraint while we hope for the best.

Attempts to head off the virus at the pass have recently taken a sharp turn. Within two days of each other, the New York Philharmonic and Nashville Symphony Orchestra shut down operations, but for different lengths of time. The former canceled everything until after the new year, and the latter closed up shop until June 2021! Now it is only a matter of time before other institutions give themselves a harsh and public reality check. No matter what the decision, artistic and financial crunches are inevitable.

Instrumentalists have an outlet for their own expression, at least. What are conductors supposed to do? About a month into the pandemic, I began receiving invitations to participate in webinars, basically to speak with other conductors from disparate parts of the world about what I was doing during this period, usually followed by questions on varying topics.

Since none of us has ever gone through anything resembling a worldwide shutdown, there is not too much wisdom I can offer. Perhaps a strike or lockout is the closest I have ever come to the current situation. As Chuck Berry sang, I have "No Particular Place to Go." The conductors all find themselves in the same situation with different implications depending on their career stage, which could be divided into three categories.

Those whose careers have been well-established over many years will have, with any luck, put away enough funds to manage for the foreseeable future. Conductors who head up orchestras, not knowing when or if they will come back, need to be prepared for any eventuality. And the youngsters of the bunch can only study, hoping that they will someday get an opportunity to step onto a podium.

Current music directors need to stay in close contact with their executive directors, managers, and artistic administrators. Fees will have to be renegotiated, even past the time when their orchestras return to full employment. If I were still in this position, I would probably accept whatever percentage cut was taken by the orchestra. If a guest conductor were unable to travel to my orchestra, and if I were free that week, I would take the date and more than likely accept the fee of the person who was supposed to be on the podium. This possibility will exist throughout the world if two-week quarantines remain in effect for international travel.

All conductors need to get creative. If you are the head of an orchestra that performs a sixteen-week season, check out the communities and cities nearby. Offer your services, should they be needed. You do not need a manager to do this, but some initiative on your part will be required. As I often say, "be assertive but not aggressive." Look for other projects that you might launch within your own home base, opportunities that might provide a little income not only for yourself but for instrumentalists as well. Use the Web wisely. Target the audience, donors, and musicians you will need for the future.

As far as the new kids on the block go, you have the roughest time of all. It is possible that you need to find temporary employment, just to keep some cash flow in place. I used to load dress racks and play in a piano bar, although not at the same time. One piece of advice is to use this time not just for score study but also for reading. One complaint I have about the younger generation of musicians is the lack of curiosity they have about their predecessors' careers. Now is the time to learn who they were, what their lives were like, how they built their careers, and what they contributed to the musical world.

It is time to be a sponge, just as you have done with the repertoire. Watch videos of conductors, especially ones in which rehearsal footage might be available. If you know some musicians and teachers who played under these maestri, ask questions. There is more to be learned from the past than the present. Take advantage of this moment in history, as it will serve you well when you are finally able to stand on a podium. Technique emerges from knowledge.

Above all, for everyone in the conducting profession, do not let yourselves be discouraged. I know that this is difficult. Not being able to present our art seems antithetical to our chosen craft. Most of you never thought that this kind of sacrifice came with the territory. We are unique, doing something that most people cannot even fathom. It has been a long road, whether you have been conducting for five years or fifty. Not only does the path continue, it also has many byways. Explore them all.

JUNE 25, 2020

> It is better to have a permanent income than to be fascinating.
>
> —Oscar Wilde

In the 1980s there was a popular television show called *The A-Team*. The leader of the group, Hannibal—not Dr. Lecter—had a motto, heard on each episode: "I love it when a plan comes together." One has to wonder what he said when it did not.

As we reach the four-month mark of the viral wars in America, several strategies have taken shape for easing restrictions, with some succeeding and others being met with a surge in cases. The separation anxieties are subsiding in Europe as arts organizations experiment with socially distanced performances but meanwhile increasing in the States as uncertainty looms. Amid the continuing protests, calls for parts of history to be dismantled, and a justice system careening ever more out of control, the United States of America might as well drop the first word of the country's name.

Everyone has been affected by COVID-19. Staggering numbers of people are unemployed, and no one as yet has come up with a way to create new industries or jobs during the crisis. It has been difficult enough for all musicians, but we mostly read of the plight of major institutions. On my mind and in my heart are those who work for minimum wages and indeed depend on a day-to-day income.

On June 19th, the *New York Times* published an article by Joshua Barone about the members of the orchestra of the Metropolitan Opera.

> "I wasn't expecting it to happen so soon," Mr. Valverde, now 25, recalled in an interview. Straight out of grad school, he found himself in the pit for Mozart's "Magic Flute."[2]

With base wages of more than $135,000 per year before the pandemic, this horn player is now in real trouble. Understandably, one plans a personal budget with that figure in mind. It is not difficult to appreciate his plight. He had no time to save up enough to get through this situation. The orchestra members across the square in Geffen Hall make even more. No one should begrudge this salary—we are talking about the finest musicians in the stratosphere of musical excellence. New York is also an incredibly expensive city. In these cases, the younger you are, the less prepared you are for the harsh realities of the profession.

Getting that dream job, at least in these times, is more like a nightmare.

But what about the musicians who are not paid anywhere near the salary of their counterparts in the big cities, for example, those who play in the Tulsa Symphony? Tulsa has been in the news recently because President Trump planned a controversial campaign rally in this location—where as many as 300 Black citizens were massacred in 1921 during a notorious episode of racial violence—on Juneteenth, a holiday commemorating the ending of slavery in the United States.

Members of the Tulsa Symphony receive compensation on a per-service basis, earning in the range of $15,000 to $18,000 per year, which they supplement by performing with other orchestras, teaching lessons, and playing church services. These hard-working musicians were already diversifying their income sources before the pandemic, but with the exception of online teaching opportunities, all of their revenue streams have dried up completely due to COVID-19. Moreover, many of them typically travel to Texas and Arkansas to play in other ensembles, and the piecemeal nature of their freelance income across state lines makes the process of filing for unemployment benefits all the more precarious.

How will the ongoing pandemic affect those in orchestras of all sizes all over this country? First, organizations rely on two factors to provide the revenue that allows musicians to perform: contributions from donors—both corporate and private—and ticket sales. The latter usually accounts for less than 35 percent of an orchestra's budget. One can apply this model to almost any musical institution, no matter the size.

Some businesses are returning to work, albeit with varying degrees of caution, but orchestras are not. Many have closed up shop until the new year, and at best, that is a wish, not a certainty. We hope that when the time comes for our concert and stage life to start up, the audiences will be socially distanced (some might say antisocial). Performances will undoubtedly begin with programs that have no intermission. We cannot have people waiting in line for drinks and using the facilities.

Realities need to be faced. Most of us will not be earning a living making music for quite a while, no matter what salary level we are at. When I work with young musicians in conservatories or music schools, I reserve about an hour of rehearsal to chat with the players. We talk about nerves, taking auditions, sight-reading, etc. Perhaps the most essential part of my presentation is about understanding that the music profession is filled with disappointments. It is a harsh world out there.

I go on to say that from these formative years in the training environment, aspiring musicians need to have alternate plans, just in case they are not able to achieve what they desire. Sometimes it might be in the form of another job within the music field, and other times it is a passion or hobby that they wish to pursue. These are not the words that budding music pros want to hear, but they ring true at this moment in time.

All of us want to put bread on the table and in our pockets. Those who have been around a while hopefully have had the foresight to anticipate this rainy day. Others did not save and are suffering. Online teaching can only go so far, and unfortunately there is not much in the world right now for those of us whose lives have been based in performance.

My advice is to take stock of the skills you possess to see if any of them can be utilized for the time being. In some ways, it may be like when you left school and struck out on your own. Many of us did things to earn money that were unrelated to our intended goals. Instead of lamenting about what you cannot do, start implementing what is possible. Do not worry about next week but do plan for the next half a year. Long-term strategies are the key to getting back to a more normalized world.

With that said, keep studying and practicing. You never know when the phone will ring or an email might come in, asking: "Are you available to play next week?" Or—as the other Hannibal said—"I'm not sure you get wiser as you get older . . . but you do learn to dodge a certain amount of hell."

JUNE 30, 2020

How did it get so late so soon?

—Dr. Seuss

Facing the facts is a rough business. Those of us in the arts are dreamers, always seeking to find what is next. But what if there is no next? We have come to an important crossroad during this pandemic that is forcing each of us to consider options that were at one time unthinkable.

These actions will have consequences not only for us in the orchestra business but also for musicians in every sector of the performing world. The possibility that our work, which has come to a standstill, might disappear altogether is slowly sinking in. Consequently, soul-searching and devising workable solutions are at the forefront of our thinking.

There are two aspects that intersect when it comes to orchestra members. One of those has to do with musicians who are entering the workforce, and the other concerns those who are leaving. Contracts in the United States are generous. They allow for tenured players to remain in their home orchestras almost indefinitely. Unlike their European counterparts, they do not have a set age for retirement. They literally can go on until God removes their job security.

Depending on the agreement, once players reach a certain number of years' service in an orchestra, not only do they collect a weekly salary but pension payments also start arriving, along with seniority pay and various increases accrued over time. They have little incentive to step down, even if their performance skills may have deteriorated. These days, very few orchestral musicians are dismissed.

In some ways, that is a good thing, as it allows a knowledgeable performer the opportunity to engage with the young musicians who come into the workforce. The other side of the coin is that this experience can have a deleterious effect. Musicians are loath to recognize when it is time to stop.

The sweeping impact of the coronavirus has forced the issue for some. With no guarantee of employment or a salary in the near future, several orchestra musicians are contemplating leaving the field. And who can blame them? If you have served enough years to receive all the benefits, but are unsure as to when that next weekly paycheck will show up, why not cash in now? Early predictions are that approximately 15 percent of current full-time musicians may very well pack up their cases by the end of their current contracts or even immediately.

Which brings us to the logical next question: Who will replace them? Auditions will be very difficult to pull off. With halls shut down, social distancing measures in place, musicians scattered around the globe, and vacancies needing to be filled, no one is certain when anything can proceed. Even if a venue is available, there will be many potential candidates who will fear flying. As I write this, you cannot travel between New York and Florida.

Earlier in this series of articles, I wrote about the necessity to stay local. But that was mostly concerning the conductors and soloists. Now it is clear that the same must apply to the orchestral workforce. Most ensembles have a list of substitute musicians who are engaged on a regular basis. There are always absences, leaves, and vacancies that require the services of alternates. Thinking ahead of the curve, orchestras should all consider hiring local players for at least the first half of the 2020–2021 season, if not the entire concert calendar.

Most people in the profession are coming to realize that nothing can move forward until there is a proven vaccine. But even when that time comes, we will not be assured of how many people will have gotten it. There are no guarantees that this will be enough. Remember how the various flu strains still stayed with us? Even some who got the shot still came down ill.

There must be guidelines, nationwide, that tell us when it will be safe to return. The earliest that will occur is just after the new year. By that time, however, orchestras will have exhausted their windows for announcing an audition schedule. It will not be until March or April when new musicians can be selected. This wipes out any new members joining ensembles for the season.

It is long-term thinking that will get us all through this wearisome time. We must recognize that orchestras will lose some musicians and will not be able to replace them quickly. Adjustments will need to be made to programming. Audiences will have to be kept informed and the donor base secured as much as possible.

When musicians do return to the stage, I anticipate that skills that go beyond artistic talent will become increasingly vital. The orchestral musicians of the next decade will be a different version of the traditional. The capacities to communicate well, understand technology, and bring innovative ideas are bound to become part of the hiring process. Understanding the full range of capabilities each person brings to the job is more important than ever.

I wish all those who choose to leave the very best. You have served the musical community well and deserve its gratitude. And for the musicians that will eventually take their place, I urge you to understand that we have entered a time when everything is changing. Take advantage of the opportunities you are afforded. Bring your very best.

JULY 5, 2020

The best doctors and medicine in the world can't save you if you don't do what you're supposed to do.

—Magic Johnson

There is a lot of information. At the same time, too little information is available. We don't know what to do with the information when we get it. Who is this information person anyway?

During the continuing pandemic, I have found myself in very strange lands, navigating the etiquette of virtual meetings, chat rooms, and even phone conferences in which I sense this odd disconnect between those I am speaking with and me. The more of these events I do, familiarity breeds acquiescence to this new set of communication tools.

Most of the time, my role is that of teacher. On other occasions, I have been in dialogue with colleagues in the conducting profession. I have also attended a couple of virtual board meetings during which I mostly sit and listen. One thing is clear in almost every case. If you cannot see the body language, the transition from one person to another is always awkward. No one knows when to speak, for fear of interrupting. This is exacerbated by intermittent distortions and delays, which lead to deadly silences with everyone waiting to see what happens next.

The role of leader falls to me when I am invited to speak to a group of people, sometimes not musicians. This is more like a lecture I might have given, which I always adjusted to the type of gathering and the audience. Many years ago, I spoke to a conference of lawyers. It was at the end of what was apparently a long day for them. My discovery was that the legal profession must have very little humor in it, as all my jokes and anecdotes fell flat. Perhaps they weren't funny in the first place.

Recently, I had the pleasure of being with a group of doctors. Most likely you do not know that in several cities, there are orchestras comprised of people who are in the medical profession. My father led one such ensemble called the Los Angeles Doctors Symphony Orchestra. My good friend Ivan Shulman is now their conductor, and he invited me to a "rehearsal." Instead of being able to play on their instruments, the members chat about music and perhaps the works they were supposed to be playing. Also included in the Zoom meeting were similarly minded folks from Boston.

It should come as no surprise to learn that a lot of medical practitioners were interested in becoming musicians when they were young before fate took them in other directions. After all, there are some correlations between medicine and music, the most obvious being that both deal with pulse. I take it one step further. A doctor is supposed to sustain the living. Musicians are able to bring the dead to life.

For this session, I primarily talked about my own life, especially those early days in LA. But one theme that I find important to stress is the wonderful world of the amateur. Many people think of this word in a negative way. Nothing could be further from the truth. It is precisely the amateur musicians who express themselves with a passion that many professionals should emulate.

My dad used to come home from rehearsals amazed that his orchestra only spoke about Brahms, Stradivari, or Horowitz. There was never any shop talk. I am not sure that I ever saw my father so energized by any other musicians. When I was going through my record library, I discovered a concert from 1961 with the Doctors Symphony Orchestra that my dad led at the old Philharmonic Auditorium. What incredible energy and commitment on the part of everyone involved.

Toward the end of my presentation, it was question time. All the queries were about music, but then I had an opportunity to ask a couple as well. The next day, I was supposed to venture out to the hospital, where my annual physical was going to occur. What precautions should I take? Most of the answers were what I expected, but one thing I learned was a slight variation on when and how to remove surgical gloves. Do it from the area above the wrist with your hand palm down to decrease the likelihood of coming in contact with your fingers as you pull the glove off.

But more instructive, as well as scarier, was the medical pros' opinions on when we might get back to how it used to be. No one ever used the word normal. They all agreed that a vaccine might appear by the new year, but they also said that it has to be completely approved by the FDA, then manufactured and distributed, which might take a couple of months. Then at least 90 percent of the population needs to be inoculated, and that could take up to three months. None of these doctors believes that we can be a fully functional society until April or May. And that projection assumes the best-case scenario.

What does this mean for musicians? As optimistic as we would like to be, we must be realistic. And in the real world, all of us must continue to practice patience. What did Randy Newman write? Oh yeah. "Baltimore. Man, it's hard just to live." And it got a whole lot more difficult for some.

As of this writing, Europe is banning Americans from traveling to most of its countries. We cannot even go from Florida to New York, and three states are prohibiting entry from the other forty-seven. I am still not sure how the virus knows to stay out.

So we all do what we can. Teaching singers and instrumentalists virtually is very difficult. Without the ability to see every aspect of the student, the capacity for correction is limited. More troubling is that no matter how sophisticated the devices being used, the sound is still being conveyed electronically. At a board meeting with the Manhattan School of Music, I proposed that a fund be set up to provide decent equipment for each student.

Every young musician already has a computer, phone, or tablet. What students also need are a good microphone and a couple of speakers. The mic on most devices is just not satisfactory. My estimate was that this should cost anywhere from $200 to $450, depending on what the student already has. And partnering with an electronics store could be a cost-saving measure.

You cannot do this with conducting. Even the baton technique looks vague over video. In the sessions I have been doing with musicians of varying ages from around the world, we mostly focus on score study. What was supposed to be a one-hour discussion of Elgar's "Enigma" Variations lasted more than twice the allotted time. One participant was in Australia and stayed up past 4:00 in the morning. Everyone had scores in hand and, for a piece that I think I know very well, there were a couple of wrinkles I was made aware of.

It seems that we can learn about music without the actual sounds. Putting it into practice is another matter entirely. No amount of preparation can adequately get any of us back into the swing of things, whenever that time comes. Keeping our minds occupied at least gives us hope. Now it is time to get back on the information highway and see if we can find that person who is guiding us through this era.

JULY 9, 2020

Music is a more potent instrument than any other for education, because rhythm and harmony find their way into the inward places of the soul.

—Plato

[This item was written five days before the Trump administration reversed its decision and was not posted, as it was no longer relevant. The contents remain valid, should there be another attempt to prevent students from coming to study in the United States.]

The attempt to look at the future just got kicked several steps backward. Seen in the broadest context, the ICE directive targeting international students is horrendous at best. Here is the summary as reported in the *New York Times* on July 7, 2020:

A directive by the Trump administration that would strip international college students of their U.S. visas if their coursework was entirely online prompted widespread confusion on Tuesday as students scrambled to clarify their statuses and universities reassessed their fall reopening policies amid the coronavirus pandemic.[3]

Let's think about this in terms of our musical training grounds. Since I am on the board of the Manhattan School of Music, I can attest that there have been numerous meetings about the impact of virtual and in-person instruction methods on the health and educational needs of the students. At the moment, music schools are contending with a policy change that requires them to maintain some amount of in-person instruction for international students, regardless of the health risks, to avoid the detrimental effect of these students being forced to leave the country. As the article in the *New York Times* explained, "International students will be required to take at least one in-person class to keep their visas when many universities are prioritizing online instruction."

Have any of us ever had to think about the definition of the word "class" when it comes to a conservatory? Of course not. Musicians tend to refer to the instruction as "lessons." They can be accomplished as a one-on-one between teacher and student or in the form of master classes with several participants and observers. A music education institution also offers other kinds of gatherings in the form of orchestral, chamber music, opera, or choral ensembles. To satisfy different state requirements, other courses need to be taken to qualify for a degree.

When I was a student, there were work-arounds. In place of what used to be called English classes, we had "Song Text and Opera Libretto." The only course I remember that even remotely represented something like primary education was history. Most of that was confined to the times when the great composers lived. In the 1960s, we did not have nearly as many students from abroad, even though Juilliard boasted some of the world's most exceptional teachers.

Today, many conservatories actively court students from abroad, setting up relationships with other music education organizations from across the globe. Between restrictions on travel both to and from foreign lands, and this latest crackdown on students, there is a crisis brewing. I cannot even begin to imagine the impact on other disciplines, especially medicine.

We are learning how to teach utilizing technology, but no one believes that this is truly the best way to work with young musicians. For the time being, there is nothing else we can do. I usually teach a couple of online webinars with conductors each week. These are devoted to taking a score and going through it, looking at the history of the work, trying to explain the technical traps, and once in a while trying to understand various interpretational approaches. With the Zoom technology, and the ability for the other conductors to ask questions either orally or in the chat window, this feels relatively normal.

What I cannot do, of course, is watch the conductors work with an orchestra. That is the key to successful instruction. The method in which a maestro communicates is an essential function of this profession. Much the same can be said of those who teach vocalists as well as instrumentalists. One needs to see the entire body in motion to help students understand what they need to correct.

The sound world is also essential. At the very least, the young musician needs a decent microphone and set of speakers. These days, everyone has cameras on their tablets, computers, and phones. Still, they cannot be moved around for the teacher to see every aspect of the student's deportment. And teachers cannot look students in the eyes, perhaps the most significant part of the communicative nature of instruction.

The simple truth is that we have no choice other than to teach in this electronic world. No longer can a teacher adjust the hand position of a pianist, correct the singer's posture, or even change how a baton is held. Perhaps those studying musicology, library work, or composition can manage. Still, the in-person options have been taken away, at least for those institutions that feel a responsibility for the health and safety of everyone.

And if there is no other option in the foreseeable future, what will we be seeing? According to the *New York Times*:

> Such changes could put foreign students' visas, known as F-1 visas, at risk under the new rules. International students whose universities are not planning in-person classes—which is currently the case at schools, including the University of Southern California and Harvard—would be required to return to their home countries if they are already in the United States. Those overseas would not be granted permission to enter the country to take online coursework here.

The financial implications are enormous, not to mention the loss of some of the most exceptional talents who might contribute to our country's cultural growth. Make no mistake. These new alterations are not being put in place because of the pandemic. That is just an excuse. The Manhattan School has all the safety precautions, including the necessary changes to dormitory and dining facilities, in place. No one will be put at risk. It strikes me as a scare tactic, one designed to discourage parents of the young musicians from allowing their children to study here.

How can we play this game to our advantage or at least level the literal playing field? Since there is no definition of what constitutes a "class," why not have a series of five-minute instructional presentations held in whatever is the largest space at the school? Adhering to social distancing measures, one group enters, listens to and watches whatever the news of the day brings, and then leaves. Five minutes after they are gone, the next group of students comes in. And so forth and so on. Everyone has had their "class," and then, if there are no in-person events scheduled that day, they go back to their home environment and continue as they have been doing since March.

You might be asking yourselves, "Well, if they are learning via the internet anyway, what is the point of actually being at the school?" My answer is that the students still have the opportunity to be surrounded, with distancing, by other musicians, a necessity in understanding what the world will be like when they enter the field professionally. And when things open up, they are already at the location where personal instruction will take place. Getting them back will take months, depriving each student of valuable learning experiences.

At the time of this posting, there are several lawsuits in the offing that challenge the new rules. Although it remains to be seen what will occur when the school sessions begin, and knowing that there is a push to reopen, the last thing that should be happening is to punish the students and schools because they have been forced into a difficult situation not of their making.

We have to be smart about how to proceed. Understanding the past is key to creating the future.

JULY 10, 2020

> The nature of the Internet and the importance of net neutrality is that innovation can come from everyone.
>
> —Al Franken

Change is not easy. It is built on a foundation of preexisting ideas that people deconstruct, rearrange, or reshape. For the short time that we have been a nation, America has tried to find the path to the future by looking back at the lessons of history.

It is human nature to seek out stability and security, and to hold on to traditions. With the tragic consequences of the COVID-19 epidemic, we are forced to tread carefully as we plot our return to that safe spot. We are staying conscious of the need to get back with an eye to the future. Perhaps we have been a little too conservative.

For the time being, many musicians have found novel ways to reach the public, whether through individual lessons, private concerts, or all manner of clever audio and video presentations. I have seen how creative we can be, considering that we are not actually creating the works that we perform.

At the same time, I have my concerns about whether orchestras are reaching the broadest communities possible. It seems as if our only viable means of communication is online. A lot of content is being presented, but has this moved the needle forward? I see the usual parade of participants that grace our concert platforms during the regular season. In the desire to hang on to the conventional concertgoer, we may be missing an opportunity.

Let's take all those young composers whose latest orchestral creations will be delayed for quite a while, stalling their careers. Why not put their names out front and center? My thought is for commissioning orchestras to ask each of these musicians to write a short piece for an individual instrumentalist. This piece would then be available for all to see and hear, provoking more anticipation for a performance of an orchestral score by this composer.

Some of my participation online has involved watch parties, video chats, and sometimes even pre-concert lectures on social platforms. Most of the musical material presented comes from performances over the past seven years or less. This seems to be the case for most orchestras. Newer is better, right?

Not really. All those broadcasts that began in the 1940s and have not been heard since are fantastic fodder for a public hungry for something different. Orchestras, small and large, usually have some audio archives that they can draw on. Concerts featuring the legends of the podium and the stars of the soloist circuit would be of high artistic value today. Many younger musicians are not familiar with several artists' names that were on the lips of every concertgoer generations ago. It is an excellent time to reconnect with the past.

This set of thoughts came to mind when I got a note from my brother, the first cellist with the New York City Ballet. I had come across a set of reissues that contained thirteen discs featuring our father as the conductor. It seems to be available only in Japan and the United Kingdom, although one can order it from the label, Scribendum Limited, and have it shipped internationally. Fred wondered if we would be getting residuals for these releases. That is when it hit me.

I propose that virtually all orchestras make as much of their recorded material available to the public for free. To accomplish this, the AFM rules would have to be deferred. Our orchestras are under pressure to cut salaries and benefits, so it is understandable that there would be objections to not receiving fees for work that was done years ago.

However, in my view, history such as this should not come at a cost. There is no one left who played in Toscanini's NBC Symphony, Stokowski's Philadelphia Orchestra, or Monteux's San Francisco Symphony. Much of their broadcast legacy can easily be found on various websites with no monetary output on the part of the consumer. But it can be made much more interesting to entice listeners with slightly more recent performances.

I have heard Bernstein's Mahler 2 with the Cleveland Orchestra, Carlos Kleiber's debut with the Chicago Symphony, and Kubelík performing Martinů with the Boston Symphony. These and thousands of other performances exist in orchestra archives. But most have not been made available to the public for various reasons. There are many of my collaborations that I have never heard, particularly some world or American premieres. The list is endless. Perhaps some of you wish you could enjoy a particular concert you attended again.

Now is precisely the time to get this material into the public's ears, and if a video is available, eyes. In some ways, it is the same thing as those musical instruments that sit in museums or private collections, going unplayed. There is no point in looking at them without hearing them, just as there is no point in having an audio treasury that no one can listen to.

Wouldn't it be fascinating to have commentary from today's conductors, composers, and orchestral musicians speaking about the value, or lack of same, of their individual performance? Listeners could have discussions through the chat function while each work is played. And why not make this an international project? Perhaps people from all around the globe will tune in to hear pieces and performances that have not been available until now.

We could rediscover those incredible symphonists from the 1930s and 1940s and explore serialism, experimentalism, neo-romanticism, and neo-impressionism. We could revisit composers once heard often who have disappeared from our orchestral radar. There are many possibilities, and they do not exist today for one reason: a lack of vision guided by monetary gain.

As mentioned, most of the musical workforce is doing yeoman's duty in holding on at a time when all levels of income have been minimized. Orchestras could potentially realize a tiny revenue stream from such a project, but using this idea as a platform for raising funds as we move forward seems a much more robust approach.

Present the past so that we may help solidify the future.

JULY 15, 2020

Please kindly go away, I'm introverting.

—Beth Buelow

As we move forward into July, it is becoming clear that we will pay a price for not listening. Right from the start of our isolation, my thoughts have been centered on what the musical world will be like when the time comes to start the regular orchestral season. I have been concerned about the ability of music directors and soloists to come to the States. Turns out that it is problematic the other way around as well.

The European Union has cracked down on its citizens entering the USA for fear of the virus being transmitted back to its own shores. Not surprisingly, given the aggressive reopening plans in some parts of the country and the lack of adherence to public health guidelines, we have experienced the highest spike in new cases of any country in the world. Some states, including New York, Connecticut, and New Jersey, are now imposing a two-week quarantine on visitors from other states with large outbreaks.

In my curiosity to see what the impact would be like in September, I looked at twenty-or-so orchestras' brochures with an eye to what might occur even if we opened up slightly. At the moment, we are theoretically not supposed to have events other than those that are socially distanced. Time after time the public is ignoring the warnings, and sometimes our officials are openly encouraging crowds to show up, with or without masks.

But what will audiences see and hear in our concert halls? We don't know yet, as no orchestra has officially announced any program alterations, even with the first concerts just two months away. You can hear the fingers being crossed as administrators and marketing departments keep waiting for the green light from above. Just go ahead as planned. Everything will be fine.

But clearly, all of that is in question. The orchestras that I investigated are dominated by music directors who are from Europe. There is nothing wrong with that. Each ensemble has to pick the person best suited to the job. The immediate problem that has caught so many organizations off guard is whether or not their conductors and soloists can get here at all.

Remember the predictions by some that the virus will just go away on its own? Apparently, somebody forgot to tell Corona to take the summer off. All that speculation about the warm weather nipping COVID-19 in the bud did not take into consideration the impact of holidays at the beach, protests in the streets, or bars and restaurants opening up too soon.

As it stands, we cannot go anywhere and no one can come here. Come September, even if we are able to travel, a two-week quarantine will be placed on individuals prior to any work that needs to be done. For many artists, this is their lifeblood. Conductors and soloists must be able to get from place to place. It would be fine if these artists resided in the place where they worked, like orchestra members. Maybe it is okay for those who have university or music school positions.

However, what makes this so complicated is that these guest artists are usually booked for back-to-back weeks in different locations. Conductor A might open his or her season in Paris but, a couple of weeks later, have concerts in New York or Los Angeles. Something has to give. The question is what do you give up? Stay with your European orchestra and not come to the States, or leave Paris in the lurch and get to the States in order to further your international career? And where do you stay for those two weeks of quarantine? Who pays for the lodging and meals? And there'd better be high-speed internet, wherever you are residing.

It is even more difficult for the soloists. There might be a recital at the beginning of the week in one or two cities, followed by a concerto in yet another place. Airport travel is somewhat restricted, depending on where you are going. Forget about going overseas right now. Perhaps younger artists are willing to chance it, but those of us who are older and fall right into the group that is most at risk are being very conservative.

As I wrote last month, organizations need to think locally. Utilize the musicians who are close by and least susceptible to exposure. There are no guarantees right now, but safety precautions must be put in place. Were just one artist, audience member, or usher to contract the virus, we go back to square one.

Crunch time is fast approaching, if it is not here already. This is not the time for last-minute surprises. It is my firm belief that two pieces of information should be made available to the artists, orchestras, and public. Tell everyone that your organization is hoping to go forward as planned. But if that is not possible, give the alternatives available, more than likely some sort of program with smaller forces. If we are still locked down, be prepared to cancel until the new year, as some orchestras have already done.

Stay positive about the work you have done to prepare for alternate scenarios, because your group has a plan. Reassure your audience that you are doing your best to accommodate them but that things remain in flux. Work directly with the artists, not just their managements. This is the time for direct contact, and with creative thinking, perhaps you just might come up with something that is unique and keeps the musical juices flowing.

Above all, remember what Douglas Adams wrote:

> It is said that despite its many glaring (and occasionally fatal) inac-curacies, the *Hitchhiker's Guide to the Galaxy* itself has outsold the

Encyclopedia Galactica because it is slightly cheaper, and because it has the words "DON'T PANIC" in large, friendly letters on the cover.[4]

AUGUST 13, 2020

You can live to be a hundred if you give up all the things that make you want to live to be a hundred.

—Woody Allen

It is now the middle of August. If ever there was a confluence of important decisions to be made, this is the time. Schools are supposed to reopen, but conflicting directives and information are making that choice difficult. The political conventions are approaching, and we don't have any idea of how they will look or sound. Protests continue to grow, and the enmity between sectors of the public and law enforcement seems greater than ever. Sports are experiencing the consequences, in some cases, of seemingly reckless behavior, thereby jeopardizing all participants.

And then there is our small world of classical music. Most orchestras were expecting to start their seasons either in September or very early October. Some have canceled all concerts until the new year, and a few have taken the entire 2020–2021 season off the books. Others are holding out until the last possible moment, with the hope that some miracle will allow them to proceed in some form.

I have been in touch with a few of my conductor colleagues who have dates scheduled soon. There are those who are fortunate to have two passports, allowing them a bit more flexibility in getting from one city to another. This seems a little strange, as it is possible to contract the virus no matter which document allows you to fly from country to country. Still, I wish them all the best in terms of safety and health.

What size orchestra and audience they face is another matter. A few European orchestras are maintaining social distancing for rehearsals and performances. There will be concerts with around 80 percent of the audience seats empty, if not all of them. The attempts to bring concerts back to life are noble but also fraught with peril.

Some American ensembles are going to give it a go with smaller forces as well. Even in states that are reporting increases in the number of cases and deaths, orchestras want to get their musicians back to work. Others are choosing to wait it out. My own schedule remains partially unknown.

At the end of September, I am supposed to go to Detroit and lead a set of subscription concerts. As of this writing, it is scheduled to occur in six weeks. But the actual season-opening programs occur the week before. The orchestra is fortunate in that it has the ability to stream all its concerts in high-definition video and audio. Making the concert a media-driven project is certainly a possibility, but they will have to determine if the full-orchestra programs are even feasible, much less if Orchestra Hall will actually open.

Following that week, the next three are also to be in the States. Two of those have been canceled, and I suspect that the third will also go away. The remainder of the year has me in Europe. Two of the orchestras have asked for reduced-orchestra repertoire. The others have not yet weighed in. We know that they are up and running in some form, so that is good news.

Getting into the European Union is another matter. At the moment, Americans cannot travel, unless they have dual citizenship in a European country. If restrictions are lifted, travelers might still be required to undergo a two-week quarantine before engaging in an activity like a rehearsal. My first scheduled dates are in Lyon, and I can certainly think of worse places to be holed up. This particular tour is quite nice, with a couple of weeks off along the way.

But how will I feel about traveling? This is a question that many people are asking. Is it worth the risk to be milling about in airports, worrying about social distancing at every turn, or trying to get used to conducting with musicians scattered about on all parts of the stage? The only trips I have taken out of the house have been to see a few doctors for regular checkups. Gladly, all looks good. I want to keep it that way.

There are plans to be made, flights to purchase, and accommodations to arrange. Since any number of different scenarios might come into play, everything has to be set up with the knowledge that there might be last-minute changes. Stress becomes a factor, and that is never healthy for musicians.

It is easy to imagine so many of my friends and colleagues having to deal with these very same matters. Add to that the anxiety about what members of their families might be feeling, and the uncharted waters seem cloudier than ever. We have to do our best to keep an optimistic outlook, but there comes a time when reality makes that impossible. The next time I write to all of you, it is most likely that many of these issues will be settled.

SEPTEMBER 1, 2020

> So much of what we call management consists in making it difficult for people to work.
>
> —Peter Drucker

Our strange journey to a destination still unknown has been a bumpy ride so far. Musicians and orchestra staff have hit a stumbling block completely unlike the shutdowns that occur with strikes and lockdowns. Somehow, most have remained optimistic, even though a few ensembles have had to close up shop for the entire season.

But on August 29, many of us received the following news, which sent shock waves to all sectors of the classical music world:

> It is with a heavy heart that, having endured a prolonged pandemic environment, we must announce that effective August 31, 2020, Columbia Artists Management, Inc. will close its doors. Throughout our 90-year history in supporting the arts and artists in New York and around the world, it's been a joy to be your advocates in your careers. We still believe in every one of you and your creations and are hopeful that the world will come back performing and creating like never before.
>
> Columbia Artists has engaged with a fiduciary to enter into an assignment for the benefit of creditors, a form of insolvency proceeding where assets are liquidated, and claims addressed in an orderly manner. We are working tirelessly to provide each

of you individual, concrete guidance on your specific situation over the coming days. In addition, we're working together with the fiduciary to see a safe place to land for your Columbia Artists relationship.[5]

In order to comprehend the significance of this announcement, it is necessary to understand the storied history of this company. Founded in 1930 by Arthur Judson, CAMI—as it came to be known—oversaw the American careers of almost all the leading conductors, singers, and soloists of the day. Through shrewd management and some strong-arm tactics, they dominated the field and remained on top right until the end.

The company's influence in the industry grew even further when Ronald Wilford, manager to the world's most prominent maestros, took over as president in 1970. Ruling with an iron fist, he kept a tight grip on the controls for forty-five years. Even though he had "retired" in 2000, Ronald remained as more than the titular head of the organization. There were small shake-ups as agents and artists came and went, but CAMI's strength remained resolute. When Wilford died in 2015, there was a power struggle, and the direction of the company became unclear.

There were other competitive agencies—small, medium, and large—however, they were also going through changes. With the decline of recording sales and the upsurge in online content, artists had to find their own ways through the minefield in order to get recognition. The managers were no longer career-builders but acted more like travel agents and schedulers.

Clearly the final straw was the virus. Since agencies operate on a commission basis, if the conductors and soloists are not working, there is no income. Moreover, CAMI played a major role in organizing orchestra tours in the States, another major source of revenue rendered moot. In the past there were few worries about profit, with artistry ruling the day. One time, the Vienna Philharmonic was brought over for a quarter of a million dollars but still managed to lose more than $100,000 on the tour. No one batted an eye.

With all that in mind, let's try and figure out what happens next. The longer COVID-19 hangs its hat in our country, the greater the danger to the artist agencies. What is singularly important to remember is that these companies are in business to make money, taking anywhere from 10 to 20 percent of the musician's fees, and this remains the only viable way for a management agency to continue to operate. There is no question that fees to artists will go down significantly. I already know this with my own dates going forward, not only in America but also in Europe. That means that the commissions will be less as well.

The larger corporations will hang on a while longer, but there might come a point at which they cannot sustain any degree of profitability. More than likely, several of the individuals who have worked for CAMI will start their own boutique agencies and bring along their clients who have a proven track record when it comes to being engaged for appearances. The real problem is for those in the middle, as well as musicians who are just beginning their concert careers.

While none of us wishes for our profession to disappear, it seems as if we are fast approaching the survival of the fittest. It is also a time when musicians have to take charge of their own futures. A more collaborative relationship between the artist and manager must occur, not one in which the musician believes that the agency can do everything for them. In turn, the organizations that hire the artists will have to become more involved in seeking out the talents they wish to engage.

At this point, some of you may be wondering what I am personally doing about management. Two years ago, just at the end of my tenure with the DSO, I decided that it was time to stop being a music director. With a couple of heart scares behind me, it was also a good idea to cut back a bit on the travel, which caused so much wear and tear on my internal system.

Instead of remaining with a large agency like CAMI, I went to a company where I am the only classical music client. Everyone else is on Broadway, in movies, and on television. We mostly work on special projects, and my assistant secures the engagements with orchestras. We plan out the next couple of years and stick rigidly to that timetable. If there is a period blocked out for Europe, hopefully dates will come in. If not, I have more time off.

I also have more room for educational events, whether working with conductors, teaching at universities, or giving speeches. But I am privileged. Age and experience have their advantages. I no longer need to focus on my career. When I conduct, my job is only to go out and make the best music possible. At one point, I did think about self-managing or perhaps just retaining a public relations consultant. Maybe that is one way today's generation of musicians can look at their futures.

One has to feel sorry for all those that have lost, and are about to lose, their jobs, whether onstage or behind the scenes. The dissolution of CAMI is a huge blow to an already pummeled musical world. We can only hope that at some point, everyone will realize that the world has changed, and with that acknowledgement, the way we approach the career path must change as well.

SEPTEMBER 15, 2020

I was never less alone than when by myself.

—Edward Gibbon

On March 11, 2020, I stepped off the podium at Orchestra Hall in Detroit. The strains of "Oh, Fortuna," as interpreted by Carl Orff in his *Carmina Burana,* were the last notes I would lead for . . . no one knew how long at the time. Earlier that evening, the governor of Michigan had urged communities to avoid gatherings of 100 or more people.

For six months, I wrote, watched television, tried to cook in a healthy manner, and avoided pretty much any contact with anybody. Yes, there were the obligatory trips for medical checkups, but for the most part, I got to know every nook and cranny of my abode. As several orchestras attempted to put on highly scaled-back seasons and others shut down until January and beyond, I was beginning to think that my next trip to the stage might not ever take place.

Then I got a message from Wendy Lea.

Many years ago, in the early years of the St. Louis Symphony Youth Orchestra, Wendy played violin in the ensemble. She indicated that she aspired to be a conductor, and I encouraged her. Giving her one of my batons apparently spurred her on, and now she is the music director of the Metropolitan Orchestra of Saint Louis. This is a group of mostly freelancers, many of whom are substitute or extra players in the St. Louis Symphony Orchestra (SLSO).

Wendy, like many of us, was getting restless and wanted to do something to allay the ennui that musicians were starting to feel. Being separated from colleagues and unable to make cohesive music was starting to take a toll. And this was especially true of those who made their livings from gig to gig, like the majority of the players in this orchestra.

My guess is that she truly thought it was a long shot, but she asked if I would be interested in participating in an outdoor concert in mid-September. Upon doing a bit of investigation into the history of the orchestra, I thought it was something that might make a tangible difference for the musicians as well as those who would be attending.

However, I had caveats. At seventy-six years old, and having undergone two heart surgeries over the last ten years, I could not afford to take any risks whatsoever. This meant that as much as possible, the proper precautions needed to be in place, including mask-wearing and social distancing. Even though this was an outdoor concert, there could be no guarantees that everyone would be safe. Missouri ranks fifth in the nation when it comes to new daily cases.

Monitoring the situation closely as the day of the performance approached, I started to feel more comfortable that any danger would be minimized. And so it was on a most pleasant day that Cindy and I packed up all the precautionary items we needed and headed out to St. Charles, about twenty minutes from where we live. This charming community, which has endured its share of flooding activity over the years, has an historic downtown area by the river from which the city draws its name.

In order to get to Frontier Park, where the concert was to take place, we had to drive on I-70, one of the interstate highways that crosses the country from east to west. A few days earlier, there had been a shooting on that very road. This drive-by saw two people fire into another vehicle that contained three adults and one child, a truly horrific act of violence and cowardice.

I thought about that as we headed west, but the real nail in the coffin occurred when I was looking at a couple of billboards that advertised an upcoming gun show scheduled to take place the week after our concert. The venue's website describes what is supposed to take place at this event: "This St. Charles gun show is held at St. Charles Convention Center and hosted by Midwest Arms Collectors LLC. All federal, state and local firearm ordinances and laws must be obeyed."

We all know what this means these days. Keep in mind that this is in the same state where a couple brandished firearms on their front porch, supposedly to keep protesters from trespassing. Nine of the people who gathered in protest were cited by the police on Friday, and the McCloskeys were charged with a felony. But everyone can go to the convention center and buy weapons for the next encounter.

We arrived at the concert site, where the always-great Christine Brewer was rehearsing some arias and songs with conductor Scott Schoonover. The orchestra was socially distanced, with string players masked and the winds separated individually by seven or eight feet each. It was a true stage, set almost at the river's edge in part of the old train station. This must have been fantastic at the turn of the 20th century.

I had proposed to conduct the Seventh Symphony of Beethoven, as most of the members of the orchestra would know the work and would have more than likely played it at some point. Not only would this be my first time conducting since the Orff back in March but it would also be a test of endurance. Even though I have been doing some exercising at home, there is still nothing like a rehearsal and concert to get the heart rate going.

Then there was the matter of the mask. This seems to be a choice that my colleagues around the country must make when leading their orchestras—to wear or not to wear. It is true that we stand more than six feet away from any musician, but in a rehearsal, one has to speak to everyone, and sometimes in a louder and more forceful voice in an outdoor setting. Any remarks to or from the musicians might violate the airspace and exceed the minimum distancing guidelines.

So masked it was. Everything had been sanitized, from the podium to the music stand. After a few introductory words to the ensemble, we started off. Outdoor concerts are always tricky, as the nature of the acoustic experience is dramatically different from an indoor hall. And with the players far apart, it is even more difficult for them to hear each other. In French, the word *ensemble* means together. We were anything but that, physically.

After a while, I got used to it, but because of the distance and everyone trying their best to stay together, tempos gradually began slowing down. More troublesome for me was the realization that I could not use all the tools available in the conductor's arsenal. At least half of my face was covered and, because the sun was shining right onto the front of the stage, I wore a hat. The general assumption is that it is the conductor's eyes that make contact and communicate with the musicians but, in reality, one's total countenance conveys the necessary information.

With my part of the single rehearsal lasting just an hour, I told the orchestra, which had done a fine job throughout, that this concert was about joy, energy, and life. It was the first time any of us had played onstage with a group in half a year. The audience would consist of people who missed live music and most likely several who had never heard an orchestra live. This was not the time to worry about details that could not be handled in the short time we had to put everything together.

There were two hours between the rehearsal and the concert. Sandwiches were brought in, and I had the chance to chat with members of the orchestra, several of whom I knew from my days as music director downtown. Catching up and telling good stories is always a part of the musical experience. Some of the tales were slightly embarrassing, at least as far as my own actions were concerned. I was always a bit of a smart ass, and sometimes these ventures into the world of humor would come back to bite me. But it was always in good fun.

At five o'clock, it looked like more than 500 people had gathered on the lawn to hear our program. At the same time, a group of protesters had assembled a couple of blocks away at the St. Charles police station. Motorcycles were roaring up and down the street adjacent to the stage. We were in the flight path of the planes taking off and landing over at Lambert Field. Just another Sunday in Missouri.

Wendy led off with a brisk account of the Overture to *The Barber of Seville*. I thought that *William Tell* might have been more appropriate, due to about two-thirds of the crowd wearing masks (*Lone Ranger* reference there, in case you missed it). Christine was brilliant, as usual. With Mozart, R. Strauss, Lehár, and a lovely version of *Somewhere Over the Rainbow*—arranged originally for her and our dear friend, the late Lynn Harrell—she captivated everyone and brought a tear or two to the eyes.

The Beethoven was exciting and full of energy. It was clear that the musicians were so happy to be doing what they were meant to be doing. I managed to get through it with the mask, and more importantly, I did both the rehearsal and the concert without utilizing a chair. The weight loss since the pandemic began seems to have reduced the pressure on my lower back.

We concluded with an arrangement of *America the Beautiful,* giving me an opportunity to conduct for Christine again. She and I exchanged stories of our work together in the past, in particular, our recording of Samuel Barber's *Vanessa* in London. She lives over in Illinois and is considered one of the St. Louis regulars.

Prior to the Beethoven, I gave a few remarks to the assembled masses. Looking out at them, it was a bit dismaying to see many people without the masks, but that was not as troublesome as the lack of space between lawn chairs. Yes, it was an outdoor event, but the virus does not recognize borders. Knowing that a few hours later, in Henderson, Nevada, there would be an indoor event where few would be separated and almost all would be without facial coverings, I was reminded of the gulf that separates society today.

What are the differences between laws, rules, and guidelines? Are any persons held accountable for violations of these directives? How much better off might we have been if everyone had followed the advice of the scientists right from the start? What ever happened to the word *United* in the States of America?

Between the shootings, protests, and gatherings, at least some of us could experience the joy of making music again. The celebratory air still did not seem quite normal. We all knew that this was a one-off rather than a regular presentation. It did, however, feel good in a cautiously optimistic way.

For the musicians and the people who attended this concert, it was as if we had come out of hibernation. But, as with the ground-hog, on this sunny Sunday, we could see our shadow. Perhaps it was time to burrow back into our homes. But unlike the chubby creature, we have no idea when we will come out.

SEPTEMBER 21, 2020

> Tell me and I forget. Teach me and I remember. In-volve me and I learn.
>
> —Benjamin Franklin

Each of us has a misgiving or two about social networking. Although as a society our daily lives have included this form of communica-tion, very rarely are thoughts expressed that offer potential solutions to the dilemmas facing our world. Once in a while, however, a social media post can trigger a set of ideas that might lead to something concrete.

While idly scrolling through the stream of criticism, advertise-ments, and messages, one post jumped out at me. A writer asked a question that went something like this: "If you had $100K to spend on programming during the pandemic, what would you do?" Since we are at the start of what will be at least a four-month delay in regu-lar concert presentation as well as the commencement of the school year, I found myself pondering how the two might come together.

In Lyon, one educational institution has a remarkable program in which a fourth-grade class in a public school devotes an entire week to music. All other curriculum is suspended for that time. The children learn some of the history of classical music as well as con-temporary aspects of the culture. A composer spends the week with the kids, and this is where it gets really interesting.

Over the course of six days—they have school on Saturday—the entire group creates a new piece of music, which is performed as the culmination of the week's effort. Often, they utilize found objects. These might be discovered at home, on the street, or even in the classroom itself. The piece is usually an organized improvisation, with the children divided into several small sets. Each section has its own role to play in the new creation.

The first time I saw this in action was well before I became music director of the Orchestre National de Lyon (ONL). During a guest conducting stint about fifteen years ago, the management of the orchestra told me about the program, and I expressed interest in observing. Fortunately, it occurred during my week with the orchestra, so I was able to experience it myself. What an inspiration! And what a difference from what we see, or more precisely, do not see, in our American schools: young people totally engaged in presenting something that they themselves have made, not as individuals but as a collective force. Music is one of only a few areas in which cooperation, listening, and creating come together. Some might call it the greater good. I prefer to leave out the qualifier.

Remembering this program, I responded to the query on Facebook with a post about how I would like to see the $100K go toward starting an initiative like this in our school system. Here is how it could work:

We know that orchestras across the country have had to cancel, postpone, or reorganize their programming until at least January. No one is doing full-ensemble repertoire and, in many cases, we are seeing small ensembles with either a limited number of audience members or none at all. We also know that even with drastic salary reductions, there are a number of players who are getting paid but are not able to practice their art.

Why not get those musicians involved in a school project? Each orchestra selects, let's say, five different public schools. The program does not necessarily need to be for fourth graders, as it is in Lyon. Perhaps slightly older children or even younger students will do. Getting into schools where there are no music programs should be a priority.

The orchestral musician and a local composer, in conjunction with a teacher at the school, devise a week of creative activities for the class. They teach a bit about history, listen to and watch recordings of different genres of music, and work on the building blocks that will become the basis of the finished compositional product. At the conclusion of the week, the work is performed, perhaps even more than once, for other students at the school as well as the parents and relatives of the kids in the class.

Based on what I observed in Lyon, this is an opportunity for students that they will not soon forget. By the time I concluded my tenure with the French orchestra, some people were coming backstage and saying that they played for me when they were in the fourth grade. It does not matter whether or not they decided to have a career in music. What they learned was the value of participation as a group in an activity that was creative and all-inclusive.

We do not even need the $100,000 proposed in the social media post to get this going. Our musicians are being employed by the orchestras in which they play, the teachers—although extremely underpaid—are at least drawing a salary, and the composer could be hired for a reasonable sum. Organizations such as ASCAP (American Society of Composers, Authors and Publishers), BMI (Broadcast Music, Inc.), and the American Composers Forum, as well as publishers that specialize in repertoire for young people, could assist in suggesting composers that would be appropriate for such a project.

For schools that are engaged in remote learning, we know that technology offers us the possibility of doing this project in Zoom-like fashion. Of course, this goes against what is a vital part of the musical experience: physical communication. But we must take the hand that is dealt and make the best of the cards we have.

After I posted a couple of sentences on Facebook, there were several responses, all more than favorable. At this point in my life and career, I am mostly past the point of being able to implement something along this line. Therefore, I gladly turn over the idea to anyone who wants to run with it. We need to use this time wisely and creatively. Let's do something special for the next generation.

This is a golden opportunity to reach into a treasure trove of young hearts and minds. Unlocking the spirit of imagination opens the world to possibilities that otherwise might go untapped.

SEPTEMBER 24, 2020

The tendency of the casual mind is to pick out or stumble upon a sample which supports or defies its prejudices, and then to make it the representative of a whole class.

—Walter Lippmann

We have a lot to discuss this time around. Arts, politics, society, and health have all intersected, at least for me. Let me begin with a decision that was agonizing but, ultimately, appropriate.

Over the course of the pandemic, I have, despite some of my written observations, tried to keep an optimistic view. Somehow, without concrete evidence to the contrary, I believed that things would be under control enough to allow me to fulfill at least one concert date that was on my calendar, namely my engagement in Detroit.

A return to my former orchestra might have sent a hopeful sign that we would eventually return to some degree of normal performance practice. Similar to a few organizations, the DSO is offering digital concerts with no audience and reduced orchestral forces. The new music director, Jader Bignamini, was able to present two weeks of livestreamed programs. If the performances felt forced or uncomfortable, he did not show it, and everything proceeded in an organized manner.

With a little over a week to go before I was to arrive in Detroit, the conductor who was scheduled to appear prior to me traveled from Europe to New York, where he has an apartment. Due to the restrictions in place in the State of New York, he was subject to a two-week quarantine, making his trip to the DSO impossible. Now the orchestra was faced with finding a conductor to step in at the last moment. As far as I knew, this was the first replacement that took place during these opening weeks among those ensembles that were up and running.

Now it was my turn. Although every safety precaution was outlined and seemingly well-defined, I still was concerned about potential exposure during this four-day trip. Should I travel by airplane as originally planned, or could I avoid more risk by making the almost-nine-hour drive? Even though the hotel where I was to stay made assurances about their cleaning protocol and air filtration, it had not yet opened up some of its amenities, including room service. Just having turned seventy-six years old weighed heavily on my mind as I considered the many issues affecting all parties.

In the end, I worried more that should Cindy and I find ourselves with any trace or symptom of COVID-19, we would feel terrible that we might have contributed to even one more case of the virus. And we would not know where or when we contracted it. With one week to go, I withdrew from the engagement. Everyone in Detroit seemed to understand, and I was confident that with a week's notice, a replacement conductor could be found.

If you were to go back and look at the very earliest of these postings, you would see that I outlined three things I thought orchestras might do to facilitate concert presentation and keep safety protocols in place. First, I suggested that using tablets instead of sheet music would make the physical act of touching the paper moot. Next, I recommended placing sound monitors onstage to help mitigate the distance factor between the musicians, something a few players have mentioned to me as a problem during rehearsals and concerts. Finally, I proposed engaging local artists to conduct the programs.

Given the likelihood of additional cancellations as the season moves forward, why risk bringing in musicians from far away when there is wonderful local talent to showcase? Wouldn't it be a fine message for orchestras to send that they are supporting local artists, both to give deserving conductors the opportunity and to enhance safety measures by eliminating those who have recently traveled from the equation? I would like to see orchestras consider this idea in the months ahead.

Just days before I made the difficult decision to stay at home, Ruth Bader Ginsburg passed away. Normally, this would be a solemn, nonpolitical event, a time for reflection on a life well-lived. But of course, it turned divisive almost immediately. It was my honor to have met her on several occasions and to hear her extol so much passion about music. Why couldn't we just let it be that way, reveling in her impact on society, whether one agreed with her or not?

No, we live in different times. It is now possible to say one thing just three or four days earlier, or four years earlier, only to reverse course and not be held accountable for those positions. This applies no matter which side of the aisle you support. It is one thing for me to change my mind about slowing down for the restatement of the chorale near the end of Brahms's First Symphony, but quite another to do or say something that has an impact on society.

Now I was thinking not only about my replacement in Detroit but, much more importantly, who would sit on the Supreme Court bench. It is unclear whether we will have eight or nine justices in place on November 3rd or January 20th. By the latter date, the majority of orchestras are hoping to be back to full strength, but that remains very much uncertain. Why?

Because earlier this week, in the space of about five hours, we got conflicting information from our own CDC (Centers for Disease Control and Prevention) as to how the virus is spread. Between the intractable positions of our politicians and the confusion being sown by the very people we are supposed to believe, how are we to know which way is up? Further compounding the dilemma is the daily roll call of organizations announcing cancellations past the new year.

None is more visible than the Metropolitan Opera, which announced that they were closing up shop for the remainder of the 2020–2021 season. At the same time, they revealed their plans for the following year, as if people were ready to make a decision to see a production on May 16, 2022. Mind you, there is no positive spin to put on the news that the most prestigious house in the country will be closed for such a long period of time. Yet artists still have to plan, budgets must be met, fundraising has to continue, etc.

What troubles me is that there are artistic matters of equal, if not greater, economic impact than the opera company. What about all the theaters, touring companies, ballet troupes, and drama organizations? Virtually every one of the seven lively arts is impacted. Meanwhile, as theaters in Europe have tried to go ahead full steam, those countries are experiencing rapid rises in new virus cases. Whether or not they can be traced back to performers or audience members might never be known.

The bigger question is what can anyone do about it? From what I have read, creativity has been at a premium, with a few companies trying out experiments that are clearly one-offs. *La Bohème*, performed as a drive-in event, is amusing and perhaps interesting one time, but that is it. The computer screen has become the epitome of Marshall McLuhan's *The Medium Is the Massage*. That seminal book from 1967 seemed almost preposterous back then, but now is eerily prophetic. For those of you who do not know it, I encourage you to get a copy or at least listen to an audio version, as it is incredibly meaningful for our time.

A few hours after learning of the Met's closure, the world was treated to the following statement by President Trump when asked if he could commit to a peaceful transition if he loses the election: "You know that I've been complaining very strongly about the ballots, and the ballots are a disaster. . . . Get rid of the ballots and you'll have a very peaceful—there won't be a transfer, frankly. There will be a continuation."

Ironically, these words were spoken less than twenty-four hours after my mail-in, absentee ballot arrived at my house. On November 3rd, I am supposed to be in France, a trip that is very much in doubt right now. In Missouri, you have the option of voting ahead of the election date. Given the amount of speculation regarding when or if our ballots will be counted, I might skip the post office and take the ballots straight to the polling station. There are several posts and initiatives that are literally up in the air in this state.

By air, I mean that on the same day the president told us that voting was a hoax, avoiding speaking about the virus, the governor of Missouri and his wife came down with the disease. After refusing to mandate anything regarding masks, Mike Parson now finds himself in the awkward position of having to defend that stance, which cost him the opportunity to participate in a debate with his opponent two days later.

Topping all of this off was the grand jury in Louisville finding no one at fault for the murder of Breonna Taylor. We do not need more unrest. People will always question what justice means. What it should not stand for is violence. Like many Americans, and perhaps others around the world, I feel as if society is collapsing all around us, and there is little that the majority of us can do about it.

Saving an opera house, streaming our concerts, voicing our opinions, and confronting an ever-divisive society seem almost impossible and, in some cases, not as meaningful as we might have believed six months ago. Still, we must press forward, hoping that our collective will might come to some sort of consensus as to what is right.

We have to be innovative. Practice safe and healthy living. Allow for celebration and mourning without interruption. Look past the near future to achieve a lasting artistic sensibility. Get out and vote. Understand that we must be judged equally under the law of the land as well as the laws that bind us morally.

I am cautiously pessimistic.

OCTOBER 5, 2020

> It can hardly be a coincidence that no language on earth has ever produced the expression, "As pretty as an airport."
>
> —Douglas Adams, *The Long Dark Tea-Time of the Soul*

One of the fingernail-biting experiences in life is watching the scoreboard as the last day of the regular baseball season approaches. Will your team get to the playoffs by winning or as a result of losses by the others?

In the meantime, there is another, more dramatic game going on. Those of us who are supposed to be traveling keep a close eye on restrictions that each country is imposing on people as they enter foreign lands. I have a seven-week tour coming up near the end of the month involving five separate countries, and the situation in each of those places has an impact on the feasibility of the other dates.

As I write this I am scheduled to step onto the first airplane in three weeks. When I decided not to go to Detroit, my concern was not the aircraft but being in such an open and public place like the airport itself. How were the bags going to be handled? What if there were delays? So Cindy and I determined that it was safer to drive.

However, upon further reflection, we realized that nine hours on the road each way was too much to handle. Any reservation on our part would not be conducive to decent music-making. We stayed home, hoping that I would get the opportunity to see all my friends in the Motor City at some point in the near future.

Europe was another matter indeed. Several countries have opened up significantly, albeit with some experiencing major upticks in outbreaks. Two of those are on my schedule. The start of the itinerary is in Lyon, which presents all kinds of obstacles. It takes three airplanes to get there from St. Louis. Some of France is in lockdown mode, but Lyon has been spared for the time being.

One has to get a special travel allowance from the government in order to enter the country. But this is only for those considered essential workers and those conducting business important to the French economy. Apparently, a conductor qualifies. I have been in regular contact with the ONL's artistic administrator, Ronald Vermeulen. We changed the program a couple of times and had to make an adjustment for a run-out concert. In Lyon, they are playing with reduced orchestra and around 1,500 people in the audience. That number had diminished by almost half upon the latest uptick in cases across the country.

It is becoming clear that a domino effect could take place. If one orchestra were to cancel, everything else on my itinerary would be affected. There does come a point at which, no matter how much you want to go, things have to give. In the case of Lyon, it might depend on what happens with the next date in the Canary Islands. Spain is also seeing a distressing spike in cases, meaning that going via Madrid carries all kinds of risks. You can never know who the travelers mingling about in the airport might be. As much as you try to sidestep and stay away from others, it is impossible to be sure.

Flight schedules have been cut to a minimum. Entry requirements are subject to review on a weekly basis, with new restrictions put into effect with little notice. But the orchestras on my itinerary have not yet canceled anything. It feels like they are letting me decide, even though getting information about what is really going on in each country is difficult.

Helsinki is my next scheduled stop, and their restrictions are pretty stringent. But the decision seems to be up to the border guards upon your arrival. They could take one look at you and your passport and turn you around. That just does not seem like a risk worth taking, and since it is in the middle of the trip, should that one fail, there is no way to complete the journey. And who knows how long it would take to get a flight home.

Berlin and Dublin follow, with the latter looking impossible and the former possible, assuming I get into Finland in the first place. Still, it seems that the best option is to wait until the end of the week and see where things are.

Now all of you get to blog watch. Will I go or will conducting have to wait until next year? These decisions are serious, and as much as I want to make music again, health and safety for everyone comes first. Meanwhile, the baseball scoreboard watch ended and miraculously, the Cardinals made it into the playoffs. COVID-19 had kept them off the field for seventeen days, and they had to make up all the games in a very short period of time. It was a grueling schedule, yet they persevered. But at the end of the series with San Diego, the schedule caught up with the birds. They managed to win Game One, but in the end, their season was over.

And now that the president and first lady have contracted the virus, perhaps there will be more awareness of what everyone should have been doing in the first place. Baseball's world series will end in a few weeks. The virus, on the other hand, will be around as long as people insist on defying the science. Musicians can only stand by and decide if they can convince others to follow the guidelines. The best any of us can do is to take care of ourselves.

OCTOBER 10, 2020

Only the guy who isn't rowing has time to rock the boat.

—Jean-Paul Sartre

In recent weeks, there has been a lot of news about orchestras settling contracts, some for up to five years. This is a very encouraging sign, as security for the musicians has been hard to calculate during this shutdown. One must hope that contingency plans are in place should the virus continue well into the new year.

The reason I am bringing this up has to do with the role of music directors as we move forward. Many of them cannot enter the States right now or are put into quarantine upon arrival. In several cases their services as conductors have not been required, as their orchestras are not working, even in reduced numbers. Perhaps some are assisting in repertoire choices for chamber music concerts.

The most important question is: "What will happen when and if orchestral seasons resume?"

In order to truly understand this query, we must examine the state of this crisis today, before we can presume to predict where things might go. The music director is the face of the orchestral institution. In the days before fifty-two-week contracts, that person would lead at least half of the performances, thereby shaping the sound and repertoire of the ensemble. This is certainly not the case today, as music directors spend around sixteen to eighteen weeks with their home orchestra. The rest of the season is turned over to guest artists, who lead classical programs as well as pops and educational concerts.

With some orchestras completely shut down, others doing programs with reduced forces, and the rest only performing without conductors, one has to wonder whether the concept of the music director really still exists. In an article published by the *Times* on October 1st, music critic Richard Morrison wrote:

> It is my contention that what the music world has gone through in the past decade, culminating in the existential trauma of coronavirus, may be the equivalent of "last orders, please" for the old-school maestro. It has certainly sounded the death knell of the word. "Among orchestral musicians, certainly in Britain, the title 'maestro' is now used only with the heaviest coating of sarcasm," says one veteran player.[6]

Most of the piece speaks about abusive behavior, dictatorial methods, and old-school preening, all things that defined many of the great conductors during the 20th century. We do live in a different time and have been moving closer to a more democratized set of orchestral norms. The music directors are chosen in concert with board members, city leaders, and the orchestral musicians themselves.

In some ways this new paradigm makes sense. If the artistic leader is not present for two-thirds of the entire season, why shouldn't those who are performing have a dominant say in who leads them? On the other hand, leaving aside the extreme behavior of earlier maestri, it is difficult to argue with the results the very best ones achieved. It was fairly easy to identify the singular orchestral personalities of Szell's Clevelanders, Toscanini's NBC, or Ormandy's Fabulous Philadelphians.

Let's say that our concert life resumes as it was, perhaps by March. For most orchestras, at least in the States, a year will have passed since the membership of the orchestras played together as a full unit. But it will also have been at least that long since the music director stood on the podium and led the entire group. How long will it take to get things back into shape? What will be the impact of incoming musicians who have yet to play one note with their new orchestra? Will the audience return, and can new listeners be found?

Mr. Morrison has some possible answers, none more interesting than this:

> [Music directors] will be prepared to live and work in the same city as their orchestra for most of the year. They will throw themselves into enthusing school pupils and grappling with the thorny question of how an orchestra makes itself relevant to everybody in the community—not just the small segment of the population that has always supported classical music.

I could not agree more, but I would take it one step further, in the interest of creating individuality. When we resume, organizations should alter what they planned for the first two months upon return. The music directors of most orchestras should spend between six and eight consecutive weeks with their home ensemble, working to create a true sonic profile, one that might have disappeared over the past year or might not have existed in the first place.

At the same time, orchestras have an opportunity to show off their creative thinking. The pandemic has caused all of us to imagine new formats, repertoire choices, and outreach initiatives. Music directors might have to go into overdrive, but in many ways, that is what they have been hired to do.

The artistic administrators have been busy moving soloists and conductors around during these last months, so they are accustomed to the chess game. Would the music directors need to give up their guest dates during this time? Absolutely. What happens to the guest conductors who were already scheduled to appear? They can fill in the slots that will now be vacant due to the music director returning to his or her home orchestra. What if the music director has two or three posts? In that case, split up the time, giving each orchestra an equal number of consecutive weeks. What about the educational programs? The music directors should conduct them to take advantage of the opportunity to engage with young people.

The reason I like this solution lies in the final sentence of Mr. Morrison's article, as quoted above. What better way to establish ties to the community than to spend a lot of time in it? Connections with board members, businesses, and the public can truly help, as we most certainly will face huge financial challenges for the foreseeable future.

This is what the old-time maestros did. There is no reason that it cannot happen again, this time with a truly cooperative spirit.

OCTOBER 19, 2020

Every step of life shows much caution is required.

—Johann Wolfgang von Goethe

During the more than half a year of pandemic shutdowns, I have spent a lot of time dwelling on what others should or should not be doing. Whether addressing matters concerning performers, administrators, or audiences, my observations and suggestions have come from the standpoint of an outsider looking in. Other than a decision not to make the nine-hour drive to Detroit to lead rehearsals and a concert, I have mostly been shielded from heeding my own advice.

Ever since it became clear that musical life was being turned inside out, I realized that a major verdict might need to be rendered as October arrived. When COVID-19 first reared its ugly head, I, like so many others, did not believe that it would affect me. Exercising every precaution, I believed that together, we could beat the virus into submission. It did not take very long to realize that this was not going to be the case.

On October 25th, I was slated to begin a seven-week, five-country European tour. The European Union seemed poised to be in much better shape than the States, having controlled the virus to manageable levels. But as the summer drew to a close, things were changing, and with the increase in cases came new sets of entry restrictions within each of the countries.

Beginning in September, I started monitoring various websites in order to get a feeling for what travel would entail. This proved almost impossible, as entry rules and flight schedules were changing on a regular basis. Many of my friends and colleagues were in the same position. We exchanged calls and emails, trying to gauge how and when we might make a decision on whether or not to travel.

In my mind, I had thought for a long time that this trip would not take place. But my heart was yearning for the opportunity to make music again. Part of me hoped that the orchestras involved would actually make this decision for me. Clearly there was local awareness, as all of them needed to change the originally scheduled programs to comply with current restrictions—no *Manfred* symphony, no Shostakovich 8, no Beethoven 9. The orchestras had adjusted their plans to accommodate smaller forces and fewer audience members.

In each case, we came up with some very nice program alternatives. Soloists had to alter their repertoire as well. There would be no intermissions. Social distancing would be in place, although each hall had its own set of rules as to how many musicians could be onstage at the same time. But it all seemed to be doable.

Then, reality kicked in.

Being based in St. Louis has so many benefits, but it also has a few drawbacks that complicate life for the itinerant musician. When I was music director, Trans World Airlines had nonstops to London and Frankfurt. Paris used to be on their schedule as well. The company went belly-up in 2001, by which point I had left the Midwest. Today, with no international flights operating out of St. Louis, one has to connect through another US city to get to Europe.

No matter how it was sliced, it would take three airplanes and four airports to get to my first destination, Lyon. During the whole seven-week trip, there would be only one occasion when I could fly directly to the city where I was to conduct. Being on the plane was not as much of a concern as spending hours in the terminals of more than fifteen airports, a prospect that seemed more ominous during this pandemic time. Cindy and I take many precautions, but there are sadly many who do not seem concerned with the safety and health of others.

What if flights were delayed? How did baggage handling affect safety? Was it really possible to make it through an eight-hour flight with heavy-duty masks in place throughout?

But that was just one part of the picture. Another consideration was the COVID testing that had to take place prior to departure, and again upon arrival, in each city, and the corresponding quarantine requirements, which varied by destination. In some cases the self-isolation timeframe overlapped with the rehearsal schedule. Moreover, we learned that in some countries the decision to grant or deny entry rested with the border guards on a case-by-case basis—there were no guarantees. Should we be turned away at the border, finding available flights to return to the United States could be difficult.

Cindy and I have been very cautious about dining out. We have only done it on two occasions, one of them outdoors and the other with a couple of good friends, in a surrounding that had about twenty people well-separated from each other. With cool and cold weather coming up during the trip, al fresco dining could not occur, and even room service might be a dicey proposition.

Perhaps if I were a younger man, it might have been possible to take these risks. Even though age is just a number, and I am in good health, I can't deny that I am in a more precarious position than my youthful colleagues. But overriding all these obstacles was the genuine fear that Cindy and I might be putting others in harm's way after a potential exposure. Stress is not conducive to good music-making.

Even though the science has been difficult to follow at times, exercising caution and prudence seemed better than relying on the observations and pronouncements from unqualified politicians.

And so it came to pass that on October 5th, I notified my European agent that it was time to withdraw from these engagements. That gave each orchestra ample time to secure the services of another conductor. Some already had a person on standby. I wrote to a couple of the orchestras' music directors whom I know to express my disappointment, and everyone seemed to understand. Hopefully these dates can be rescheduled sometime in the next year or two.

With the exception of a couple of appearances in front of a virtual audience in St. Louis, the next time I am scheduled to lead a full concert is New Year's Eve. We do not know how the situation will unfold as this disaster-filled 2020 comes to an end, but at least looking forward to better times provides a sense of hope. In the meantime, all of us have to do our best to stay safe, healthy, and sane.

The first two tasks are easier than the last one.

JANUARY 6, 2021

> You can't fix yourself out of a mental health issue. You can't wake up and say, "Today I'm not being depressed!" It's a process to get well, but there is recovery.
>
> —Margaret Trudeau

When I received a request from violinist Holly Mulcahy to write about what music we might use to improve mental health as we cope with the pandemic, I focused my attention on the words she used to describe our possible emotions ("anxiety, sadness, fear, anger, manic energy, lack of motivation") as well as her directive: "pick a single work that reflects and supports that emotion, and then pick a secondary work that alleviates that feeling just a notch up or down."

Hmm . . . that was a tough one. Were the musical remedies limited to the world of classical music? How could one really choose just one emotion? Was this request adding to the already burdensome weight of isolation?

Actually, for me, it has not been all that bad. At age seventy-six, I have been contemplating cutting back anyway. What better time to assess my options for the future? I have finished writing my third book, started a fourth, become a pretty decent heart-healthy chef, and discovered all kinds of movies and TV series to keep me occupied.

But I have also spent a good deal of time in my music library pouring over scores I have performed and others that have sat on the shelves for decades. In the process, I expanded my musical world. So I put on my thinking cap and tried to envision what might be an acceptable answer to Holly's query.

One of the most frequently asked questions of musicians, and one that we always have to dodge, is: "What is your favorite piece of music?" Of course, there is no single answer to this. Everything depends on the occasion, time of day, and general mood one is in. My retort takes the form of two responses: "Whatever piece I am conducting at the moment," or "Anything by my wife." The first answer works on all occasions, and the second works best when Cindy is around to hear me say it.

But I can think of one piece that applies in virtually any circumstance. I know this violates Holly's dictum to pick one work that reflects a single emotion and a second piece to alleviate that feeling, but my choice is Aaron Copland's *Appalachian Spring*.

Why?

Because, at least in the twenty-minute suite, it contains all the emotions and sense of recovery that we need at this time. I look at things from a very American perspective, and Copland's score has that one characteristic we all share: cautious optimism. It begins simply and quietly, then moves into a folk-like dance followed by music of unbearable tension and sorrow. After that, we get to another light-hearted dance and some good old-fashioned country fiddlin'. A short reference back to the opening music brings the slightly aggressive building-of-the-house music. Then we are taken to the mountains and the Shakers, who sing the hymn *Simple Gifts*, which is followed by a set of variations. The triumph of spirit is short-lived, as it is time to reflect on all we have seen and heard.

The coda provides one of the most beautiful and satisfying conclusions of any piece of music I know. Sparsely orchestrated, it is a prayer of Thanksgiving, which gives way, once again, to the opening of the piece. A final, indefinite chord in the strings—a C-major chord is overlayed with a G-major triad—is punctuated with the unison of three notes played on the glockenspiel and harp. Our journey is complete, but we are left with the feeling that there is still more to experience.

Isn't that perfect for this time?

But I guess I should really deal with what Holly requested. Of course, I am going to do it in a different way. Here goes:

- Anxiety: No other choice than the variations from Bernstein's Second Symphony ("The Age of Anxiety")
- Sadness: Not the Barber Adagio, but instead, any movement from Górecki's Third Symphony
- Fear: "Gnomus" from Mussorgsky's *Pictures at an Exhibition*
- Anger: The Third Movement from Shostakovich's Eighth Symphony
- Manic energy: Christopher Rouse's *The Infernal Machine*
- Lack of motivation: The final movement of Vaughan Williams's Sixth Symphony

Maybe I should program them as a suite.

Okay, now to get us out of this depressing group, I suppose that we need to find some light at the end of the tunnel, so here are a couple of excerpts that can lead the way:

- Ravel: The first part of the *Daphnis and Chloé*, Suite No. 2
- R. Strauss: The opening few minutes of *An Alpine Symphony*
- Ginastera: Malambo from *Estancia*
- Anderson: *The Waltzing Cat*
- Beethoven: The third movement of the String Quartet in A Minor, op. 132
- Oscar Peterson or Michel Camilo: Any up-tempo track

Quite a journey. These selections will not have the same result for everyone. If you wish to try one of the musical medications, pick carefully. They certainly work for me.

As we emerge from our isolation and come to grips with a new reality, it will be important to remember what we have all experienced and to move forward with a sense of Copland's cautious optimism.

CODA

And in real life endings aren't always neat, whether
they're happy endings, or whether they're sad endings.

—Stephen King

So many subjects, only so many words. Every time I completed
a chapter it seemed as if three or four other topics leapt into my
mind. In fact, I wrote several sections that were more light-hearted—
filled with anecdotes, stories, and tales. After a while, though, it became clear that they were not really appropriate for this book.

But they did get me started on another volume. While waiting
for responses to the various chapter summaries, I began to compile
information, particularly from my youth, that might make up a different kind of book than the others I have written. Early on, in my
high school days, I thought that the short story might be an effective
way for me to communicate. I started on a couple recently, and I
have found that although they are quite different in writing style, I
can still keep my own voice in this format. Time will tell whether
or not I will complete this project.

In the meantime, I have also had a chance to reflect on what is
contained in this publication. During the period between editing and
printing, several of the subjects I have addressed in the book were
already being discussed, but not because I had written anything. The
musical world moves quickly when it comes to looking at issues it
must confront. The problem is that only a few musical organizations
actually take the big steps necessary to effect change.

We come into the discourse late. When the diversity issue is front and center, we spend way too much time talking about solutions rather than taking bold action. When we come up with potential remedies, they tend to be for the short term. Our health concerns have been discussed for years, and yet the same complaints that were in front of us fifty years ago persist. The list could go on and on.

Having relinquished my role as a music director, it is now possible for me to express my own feelings on these subjects a bit more freely than I could in the past. One of my uncles once told me that his goal in life was to get to the point that he could laugh at everyone. I am not quite that cynical. Rather, my desire is to say and write what I wish, and at the same time, I hope that some of my words spark an active response.

This might provoke some to wonder why I did not speak with the same candor earlier in my career. As a music director, one has to dance a little and play some games. These can be with the board, management, and orchestra. A music director is part politician, diplomat, parent, psychiatrist, cheerleader, and team player. Each organization is different, but the boundaries are the same. As often as I got in trouble for what I said, there were at least ten times as many occasions when I stayed quiet.

If and when we emerge from the pandemic, come to terms with meaningful diversity in all our sectors, and halt the society of divisiveness, perhaps levelheaded minds will prevail. Even though every orchestra is bound to its own community, there are commonalities that unite us. Healthy dialogue can lead to positive results if people are willing to put in the time and effort. We need to be finished thinking about how things were and focus on how they can be.

My love for music has been the driving force in my life. Finding ways to spread the word, in particular for so-called classical music and jazz, has been a passion. What you have read here was written in the hope that it spurs discussion, debate, and action. In any event, the music must continue to speak for all of us.

NOTES

CHAPTER 1

1. Richard Strauss, "Reflections and Recollections," *Tempo* 12 (Summer 1949): 13–19, doi:10.1017/S0040298200042789.

2. One summer, while I was leading concerts with the Chicago Symphony at Ravinia, my friend James Conlon had a performance in between my Thursday and Saturday concerts. I asked if I could leave my clothes in the dressing room rather than take them back to the hotel. When I arrived for the Saturday show, however, everything was there except my shoes. It seemed Jimmy wore the same brand and took mine home after his Friday night concert. I had to go onstage with my worn-out casual footwear that evening.

CHAPTER 2

1. Marc Gordon, "On Orchestral Identity," comment submitted July 1, 2020, https://www.leonardslatkin.com/commentary/on-orchestral-identity.

CHAPTER 3

1. Karl Aage Rasmussen and Lasse Laursen, "Orchestra Size and Setting," in *The Idiomatic Orchestra* (2014), http://theidiomaticorchestra.net.

CHAPTER 5

1. Walter Tomaszewski, Facebook, June 25, 2020, https://www.face-book.com/MaestroLeonardSlatkin/posts/3183215548401044.

CHAPTER 7

1. Blair Tindall, "Call Me Madame Maestro," *New York Times,* January 14, 2005, https://www.nytimes.com/2005/01/14/arts/movies/call-me-madame-maestro.html.
2. Anthony Tommasini, "To Make Orchestras More Diverse, End Blind Auditions," *New York Times*, July 16, 2020, https://www.nytimes.com/2020/07/16/arts/music/blind-auditions-orchestras-racc.html.
3. Norman Lebrecht, "Leonard Slatkin: How to Make Our Orchestras More Diverse," *Slipped Disc,* July 16, 2020, https://slippedisc.com/2020/07/leonard-slatkin-how-to-make-our-orchestras-more-diverse/.

CHAPTER 8

1. David Prudent, "On Soloists," comment submitted July 15, 2020, https://www.leonardslatkin.com/commentary/on-soloists.

CHAPTER 10

1. Kerry Hannon, "Is It Time to Abolish Mandatory Retirement?," *Forbes*, August 2, 2015, https://www.forbes.com/sites/nextavenue/2015/08/02/is-it-time-to-abolish-mandatory-retirement/.
2. Janet Horvath, email to Leonard Slatkin. Janet Horvath is the author of *Playing (Less) Hurt: An Injury Prevention Guide for Musicians*, http://www.playinglesshurt.com.

CHAPTER 14

1. Etienne Abelin, "On Performance Practice," comment submitted July 2, 2020, https://www.leonardslatkin.com/commentary/on-performance-practice.

CHAPTER 15

1. Tim Franklin, "On Rehearsing," comment submitted July 6, 2020, https://www.leonardslatkin.com/commentary/on-rehearsing.

2. Paula Akbar, "On Rehearsing," comment submitted July 6, 2020, https://www.leonardslatkin.com/commentary/on-rehearsing.

CHAPTER 17

1. Raymond Leppard, *Raymond Leppard on Music: An Anthology of Critical and Personal Writings*, ed. Thomas P. Lewis (White Plains, NY: Pro/Am Music Resources, 1993), 17.

CHAPTER 18

1. Janet Horvath, "A Musician Afraid of Sound: How a Professional Cellist Learned to Live with a Career-Ending Ear Injury," *Atlantic*, October 20, 2015, https://www.theatlantic.com/health/archive/2015/10/a-musician-afraid-of-sound/411367/.

CHAPTER 20

1. Tim Franklin, "On Education," comment submitted June 9, 2020, https://www.leonardslatkin.com/commentary/on-education.

2. "A New Deal for the Arts," National Archives and Records Administration, accessed November 30, 2020, https://www.archives.gov/exhibits/new_deal_for_the_arts/text_introduction.html.

3. Ferdinand Ries, quoted in Michael Hamburger, ed., *Beethoven: Letters, Journals and Conversations* (New York: Anchor Books, 1960), 29–30.

4. Christian Baldini, "Beethoven: Symphony No. 3 'Eroica' Opening Comparison (35 Performances)," YouTube, July 3, 2020, https://youtube/gbfaI5h0ZWc.

CHAPTER 21

1. ArtsInteractive, creators of Music in the Air (MITA), https://www.artsinteractiveinc.com.

2. Joshua Barone, "Opera Has Vanished. So Have Their Dream Jobs at the Met," *New York Times,* June 19, 2020, https://www.nytimes.com/2020/06/19/arts/music/met-opera-orchestra-jobs.html.

3. Miriam Jordan, Zolan Kanno-Youngs, and Dan Levin, "Trump Visa Rules Seen as Way to Pressure Colleges on Reopening," *New York Times,* July 7, 2020, https://www.nytimes.com/2020/07/07/us/student-visas-coronavirus.html.

4. Douglas Adams, *The Hitchhiker's Guide to the Galaxy* (New York: Harmony Books, 1979), 3.

5. Columbia Artists, email to author, August 29, 2020.

6. Richard Morrison, "Overpaid, Oversexed, Over the Hill—Has the Maestro Had His Day?," *Times,* October 1, 2020, https://www.thetimes.co.uk/article/overpaid-oversexed-over-the-hill-has-the-maestro-had-his-day-zgjb8slx0.

INDEX

Brewer, Christine, 202, 204
Brian, Havergal, 131
Britten, Benjamin, 69
Bruckner, Anton, 44;
    Ninth Symphony of, 130;
    Second Symphony of, 92
Broadway, 35–36, 41, 54, 91, 146,
    173, 199
Browning, John, 72
Buckley, Betty, 36
Buelow, Beth, 192
Buffalo Philharmonic Orchestra, 98
Bugs Bunny, 34
Bonaparte, Napoleon, 152–54

CAMI. *See* Columbia Artists
    Management Incorporated
Camilo, Michel, 222
cancellations, 72, 100, 161, 168, 175,
    194, 195–97, 206, 209–10, 213–14,
    220
Capitol Records, 34
Carlos, Wendy, 109–10
Carmina Burana (Orff), 161, 200, 202
Carnegie Hall, 32, 53, 68, 92, 112
Carousel, 36
Carter, Elliott, 131
Caruso, Enrico, 68, 95
Castelnuovo-Tedesco, Mario, 69
CDC (Centers for Disease Control and
    Prevention), 210
Chekhov, Anton, 45
Chicago Symphony Orchestra (CSO)
    16, 17, 19, 20, 39, 40, 42, 50, 51,
    191, 227n1.2
Chisholm, Shirley, 57
Chopin, Frédéric, 125
Cincinnati Symphony Orchestra, 39,
    42
Classic 107.3 FM: The Voice for the
    Arts in St. Louis, 133
Cleveland Orchestra, 18–19, 39, *42*,
    191, 216

Clinton, Chelsea, 39
Cobain, Kurt, 115
Colgrass, Michael, 131
collective bargaining agreements,
    27–28, 76, 98, 116–17, 124–26,
    128, 180
Columbia Artists Management
    Incorporated (CAMI), 50, 52,
    53–54, 197–200, 230n21.5
Columbia Records, 96
composers, 101–107, 129–34;
    advice for, 105–107, 147;
    American, 16, 41–42, 44, 77–78,
        92, 130–32;
    as conductors, 69;
    contemporary, 93, 102, 104–105,
        117–19, 131–33, 190;
    during COVID-19, 167, 192;
    as educators, 205–207;
    female, 64–65;
    of film scores, 32–34, 69;
    interactions with, 104–105, 117–19,
        157;
    respecting, 19, 21, 25, 73–74, 94,
        104, 107, 113, 125;
    as soloists, 67–68;
    young, 133, 176, 190
Conant, Douglas, 143
concertos, performances of, 1, 21,
    34–35, 67–74, 115, 116–17, 123,
    125, 146, 194
conductors:
    advice for, 7–13, 115–20, 132, 147;
    American-born, 19–20, 39–45, 91;
    as collaborators, 35, 70–74, 119;
    communication skills of, 12, 35, 41,
        91, 160, 173, 187;
    as composers, 69;
    during COVID-19, 160, 173,
        175–77, 185, 187, 193–97, 203,
        215–17;
    as interpreters, 21, 33, 37, 93, 101,
        104–105, 110–13, 187;